# The Duchess of Windsor

# The Duchess of Windsor

## Diana Mosley

Editorial Consultant
and Illustrations Editor:

## Jack Le Vien

The more alive one is,
the more one is attacked.
*Yeats*

SIDGWICK & JACKSON

LONDON

*A number of the photographs in this book came originally from the private collection of the Duke and Duchess of Windsor, and the publishers are grateful for the Duchess's permission to use them.*

First published in Great Britain in 1980
by Sidgwick and Jackson Ltd. in association
with the K. S. Giniger Company, Inc.

The insignia reproduced in this book was
adopted by the Duchess and uses three
intertwined 'W's for Wallis Warfield Windsor.

Designed by Ray Hyden
Picture Research by Anne-Marie Ehrlich

*A Ballade of the First Rain*, G. K. Chesterton
*Afterthoughts*, Logan Pearsall Smith (Constable & Co. Ltd.)
*Eurydice*, Edith Sitwell (the Estate of Edith Sitwell and Macmillan Publishers Ltd.)
*The River Song*, Ezra Pound (Faber & Faber Ltd.)

ISBN 0 283 98628 X

Printed and bound in Great Britain by
William Clowes (Beccles) Limited
Beccles and London

for Sidgwick and Jackson Limited
1 Tavistock Chambers
Bloomsbury Way
London WC1A 2SG

# Contents

|  | Acknowledgements | 6 |
|  | List of Illustrations | 7 |
|  | Foreword | 11 |
| I | A Young Lady from Baltimore | 12 |
| II | Navy Wife | 22 |
| III | The Little Prince | 29 |
| IV | Prince of Wales | 40 |
| V | Divorce and Re-marriage | 49 |
| VI | Ich Dien | 58 |
| VII | Mrs Simpson meets the Prince | 68 |
| VIII | The Prince in Love | 74 |
| IX | Loved by a King | 85 |
| X | Storm Clouds | 96 |
| XI | Abdication | 104 |
| XII | King into Duke | 115 |
| XIII | Marriage | 125 |
| XIV | The First Two Years | 140 |
| XV | War | 150 |
| XVI | The Bahamas | 163 |
| XVII | The Windsors in France | 169 |
| XVIII | The Brilliant Duchess | 188 |
| XIX | Old Age | 198 |
| XX | Summing Up | 211 |
|  | Index | 220 |

# Acknowledgements

I am very grateful to the following, who have given me invaluable help in writing this book: Jane, Lady Abdy; Mrs Herbert Agar; the late Sir Cecil Beaton; Lady (Rex) Benson; Ann-Mari Princess von Bismarck; Mâitre Suzanne Blum; Comtesse René de Chambrun; Father Jean-Maria Charles-Roux; The Lord Colyton; Grace, Countess of Dudley; Sir Dudley Forwood Bart; Mme Jean Gaudin; Dr Henry Gillespie; Marquis de Givenchy; Mr John Grigg; Mr Horst; Mr James Hudson FRCS; Mrs James Hudson; Mr Geoffrey Keating; Mr Walter Lees; The Lady Elizabeth Longman; Prince Jean-Louis de Lucinge; Miss Rose Mary Macindoe; Mrs McLaughlin; Mme Igor Markevitch; Mrs Metz; M. Hervé Mille; Major-General the Viscount Monckton of Brenchley; The Hon. Rosamond Monckton; Sir Berkeley Ormerod; M. Gaston Palewski; Miss Fiona Da Ryn; M. Maurice Schumann; The Countess of Sefton; Miss Monica Sheriffe; Professor Robert Skidelsky; Mr John Utter; Mrs Diana Vreeland; Miss Margaret Willes. My special thanks to Lady Lloyd, who allowed me to quote from an unpublished memoir written shortly before his death by her uncle, Captain the Hon. Bruce Ogilvy, who was equerry to the Prince of Wales for nine years.

I should also like to thank the following for permission to publish extracts from copyright material in their possession: Allen & Unwin Ltd for *Queen Mary, 1867–1953* by James Pope-Hennessy (1959); W. H. Allen & Co. Ltd for *The Woman he Loved* by Ralph Martin (1974); Jonathan Cape Ltd for *The Slump* by John Stevenson and Chris Cook (1977); Cassell & Co. Ltd for *A King's Story: The Memoirs of H.R.H. the Duke of Windsor* (1951); Collins & Co. Ltd for *Diaries and Letters 1930–9* by Harold Nicolson (1966); Constable & Co. Ltd for *Winston Churchill: The Struggle for Survival* by Lord Moran (1966); Evans Brothers Ltd for *Your Dear Letter: Private Correspondence of Queen Victoria and the Crown Princess of Prussia, 1865–71* edited by Roger Fulford (1971); Eyre & Spottiswoode Ltd for *Editorial; The Memoirs of Colin R. Coote* (1965); Hamish Hamilton Ltd for *Victor Cazalet* by Robert Rhodes James (1976); Hart-Davis MacGibbon Ltd for *The Light of Common Day* by Lady Diana Cooper (1959); Michael Joseph Ltd for *The Heart has its Reasons* by the Duchess of Windsor (1965); La Pensée Universelle for *Mon Dieu et mon Roi* by Jean-Maria Charles-Roux; Macmillan Publishers Ltd for *Life with Lloyd George* by A. J. Sylvester (1975); and the Earl of Airlie for *Thatched with Gold* by Mabell Airlie (1965).

**Page**

10 A portrait of Wallis Simpson, taken by Cecil Beaton, 1936 (*Sotheby's Belgravia*)
14 Teackle Wallis Warfield (*Edward L. Bafford Photography Collection, University of Maryland Baltimore Library*)
14 Wallis' birthplace, Blue Ridge Summit, Pa. (*Maryland Historical Society*)
15 Alice Montague Warfield, with her daughter, Wallis (*United Press International*)
16 Wallis with her grandmother (*United Press International*)
17 Wallis as a schoolgirl (*United Press International*)
17 Oldfields, Baltimore (*Hughes Co. Commercial Photography, Baltimore*)
18 Wallis as a debutante (*United Press International*)
18 Wallis in 1915 (*United Press International*)
20 Lieutenant Earl Winfield Spencer
20 Wallis at her marriage to Lieutenant Winfield Spencer, 12 November 1916
25 Wallis as a young naval wife, Coronado (*United Press International*)
25 Don Felipe Espil
25 Wallis in 1928 (*Keystone Press*)
28 Four generations of British monarchy, 1894 (*Associated Press*)
33 York Cottage, Sandringham (*Radio Times Hulton Picture Library*)
33 The infant Prince Edward, with his mother and grandmother (*Keystone Press*)
35 Prince Edward with his brothers and sister, 1903 (*Popperfoto*)
36 Prince Edward, with his brother Bertie, 1912 (*Popperfoto*)
37 Prince Edward in naval uniform, 1913 (*Popperfoto*)
42 The investiture of Edward as the Prince of Wales, 1911 (*Central Press Photos Ltd*)
42 Prince Edward visits France, 1912 (*Radio Times Hulton Picture Library*)
43 The Prince of Wales, 1914 (*Popperfoto*)
46 The Prince with George v, France, 1915 (*John Topham Picture Library*)
51 Two photographs showing Shanghai in the 1920s (*Popperfoto*)
52 The British Legation, Peking (*Popperfoto*)
52 A Temple on the Tartar Wall, Peking (*Popperfoto*)
54 Wallis' mother, Alice (*United Press International*)
56 Ernest Simpson (*Popperfoto*)
59 The Prince of Wales and Winston Churchill, 1919 (*Popperfoto*)
60 The Prince of Wales, Annapolis Naval Academy, 1919 (*Popperfoto*)
60 The Prince of Wales, USA, 1919 (*Popperfoto*)
65 Mrs Dudley Ward (*Popperfoto*)
66 The Prince of Wales riding in a point-to-point, 1924 (*Popperfoto*)
66 The Prince of Wales after his fall from 'Little Favourite' (*Popperfoto*)
69 Wallis in her London flat (*Popperfoto*)
69 Wallis in the dress she wore when presented at Court (*Popperfoto*)
72 The Prince of Wales and Lady Astor, playing golf (*Popperfoto*)
72 The Prince playing the bag-pipes (*Popperfoto*)
75 Fort Belvedere (*Central Press Photos*)
75 The Prince in the gardens at the Fort (*Popperfoto*)
76 A tea party at Fort Belvedere, 1934
76 Thelma, Lady Furness (*Radio Times Hulton Picture Library*)
80 The Prince with Wallis at Biarritz, 1934 (*Keystone Press Agency*)
80 The skiing party at Kitzbühl, 1935 (*Popperfoto*)
82 King George v's Silver Jubilee, May 1935. Going to a thanksgiving service in St Paul's Cathedral (*Popperfoto*)
83 More modest celebrations in a Stepney backstreet (*Popperfoto*)

87   Debutantes being presented to the King, Buckingham Palace, 1936 (*Popperfoto*)

87   The Garter King of Arms proclaims the accession of Edward VIII (*Popperfoto*)

88   Edward VIII presenting colours (*John Topham Picture Library*)

88   King Edward VIII

91   Wallis with her Cairn terrier (*Popperfoto*)

92   Wallis and the King at Pompeii

92   Wallis and the King with Kathleen Rogers at Portofino

93   Lunch aboard the *Nahlin*

93   Wallis on the bridge of the *Nahlin* (*Popperfoto*)

97   Theodore Goddard (*Messrs Theodore Goddard & Co.*)

97   The King and Wallis entertaining at Balmoral (*Popperfoto*)

99   Wallis with her aunt, Mrs Merryman, at Fort Belvedere, 1936 (*Popperfoto*)

99   Edward VIII at the State Opening of Parliament, 1936 (*Central Press Photos Ltd*)

102   Stanley Baldwin visits the Fort

105   The King visits the South Wales coalfields, 1936 (*Popperfoto*)

108   Stanley Baldwin leaving No. 10 Downing St (*Radio Times Hulton Picture Library*)

108   Lord Beaverbrook (*Radio Times Hulton Picture Library*)

110–111   A montage of press cuttings

112   Wallis with Inspector Evans, leaving their hotel in Rouen (*Keystone Press*)

117   Walter Monckton (*Radio Times Hulton Picture Library*)

117   Lord Brownlow, Katherine Rogers, Wallis and Herman Rogers in Cannes (*Popperfoto*)

120   The farewell broadcast, Windsor Castle (*Associated Press*)

120   The instrument of Abdication (*Popperfoto*)

120   Edward leaving Windsor after the Abdication speech (*Keystone Press*)

123   Cosmo Lang, Archbishop of Canterbury (*Radio Times Hulton Picture Library*)

126   Major 'Fruity' Metcalfe and Lady Alexandra Metcalfe (*Radio Times Hulton Picture Library*)

130   Château de Candé (*Sir Dudley Forwood*)

131   Wallis and Katherine Rogers at Candé (*Sotheby's Belgravia*)

132   Wallis and the Duke of Windsor reunited at Candé (*Keystone Press*)

133   The wedding of Wallis and the Duke of Windsor, Candé, 3 June 1937 (*Popperfoto*)

134   On the balcony steps at Candé (*Sir Dudley Forwood*)

134   The wedding breakfast, with Walter Monckton and Major Metcalfe (*Sir Dudley Forwood*)

135   Rev. Anderson Jardine's prayerbook (*Radio Times Hulton Picture Library*)

137   The world press at the gates of the Château (*John Topham Picture Library*)

141   The Duke and Duchess on their honeymoon, 1937 (*Keystone Press Agency*)

142   Wasserleonburg Castle (*Radio Times Hulton Picture Library*)

142   A lunch party at Wasserleonburg, June 1937 (*Sir Dudley Forwood*)

145   The Duke and Duchess in Germany, 1937 (*Popperfoto*)

146   The Duke and Duchess being welcomed by Hitler (*Popperfoto*)

147   The Duke and Duchess leaving the Berghof (*Popperfoto*)

151   The Château de la Croë at Cap d'Antibes (*Radio Times Hulton Picture Library*)

152   Cecil Beaton's photograph of Wallis, 1938 (*Sotheby's Belgravia*)

156   The Duke and Duchess of Windsor on the HMS *Kelly* (*Popperfoto*)

158   The Duke arriving at the War Office in Whitehall (*Popperfoto*)

159   The Duchess of Windsor as an officer in the French Women's Ambulance Corps (*Keystone Press*)

159   The Duke of Windsor inspecting the front, France 1939 (*John Topham Picture Library*)

164   Government House, Nassau (*Bahamas Tourist Office*)

164   The Duke of Windsor taking his oath of office as Governor of the Bahamas (*Popperfoto*)

166   The Duke and Duchess visiting survivors of a sea rescue (*Bahama News Bureau*)

166   The Duchess as President of the Bahamas Red Cross Association (*Popperfoto*)

170   The Duke with his mother, Queen Mary (*Popperfoto*)

171   The Duchess at the Paris Horse Show, 1949 (*John Topham Picture Agency*)

173   The Duke with Sir Winston and Lady Churchill after the war (*Popperfoto*)

174   The Duke and Duchess at Portofino (*Radio Times Hulton Picture Library*)

176   The Moulin de la Tuilerie in the Vallée de Chevreuse (*Columbia Pictures Corporation*)

177 The Duke and Duchess at the Mill (*Condé Nast Publications Inc. Photo by Patrick Lichfield*)

178 Sidney, the footman, with some of the Duke's pugs (*Condé Nast Publications Inc. Photo by Horst*)

182 The Duke golfing at Deauville (*Popperfoto*)

184 The Duke and Duchess of Windsor, 1951 (*Popperfoto*)

184 The Duke and Duchess of Windsor with Jack Le Vien, 1964

185 The Duke and Duchess dancing at the Hotel Plaza, New York (*John Topham Picture Library*)

186 Jimmy Donahue with the Duke at Portofino, 1953

189 The Duchess in her drawing room in Paris (*Photo by Horst*)

190 The Duchess of Windsor in the early 1950s (*Photo by Horst*)

193 The Duke and Duchess of Windsor with the Queen Mother (*Keystone Press*)

194 The Duchess in 1959 (*Keystone Press*)

196 The Duke of Windsor with Lord Monckton, 1955 (*S & G Press Agency Ltd*)

196 The Duchess and the Duke (*The Press Association Ltd*)

199 The Duchess and the Duke leaving the London Clinic (*Associated Press*)

200 The Duchess as godmother to the son of Henry and Linda Mortimer, 1969

202–3 Queen Elizabeth II, the Duke of Edinburgh and Prince Charles with the Duchess of Windsor (*Syndication International Ltd*)

204–5 The widowed Duchess with the Queen Mother after the Duke's funeral

206 The Duchess watching the return of the procession from Trooping the Colour (*Keystone Press*)

208 The Duchess returning to France after the Duke's funeral (*Keystone Press*)

208 A dinner party given by the Duchess in Paris in 1975 (*Princess von Bismarck*)

213 Wallis and the King in 1936

215 The Duke and Duchess on their wedding day

216 The Duke and Duchess on their yacht at Portofino (*Keystone Press*)

219 The Duke and Duchess in Baltimore, 1959 (*Maryland Historical Society*)

# Foreword

Der du, ohne fromm zu sein, selig bist!
Das wollen sie dir nicht zugestehn
*Goethe*

At a dinner party in Paris in the nineteen-sixties somebody asked the question: 'What would you wish for if you could have one wish?' Variations on the theme of health and wealth as a means to happiness followed, with the accent on wealth. The Duke of Windsor was one of the guests; he remained silent until prodded by the Duchess. 'Tell us what you would wish for?' she said.

'You,' was the reply.

Nobody who knew them doubted that this answer was simply the truth. She was all the world to him. They had been married for upwards of thirty years, and the drama of their marriage had faded into an historical happening from before the war. The brother who had succeeded him had been a popular King; his niece an even more popular Queen. A cynic might suggest that the Duke of Windsor was obliged to count the world well lost for love, since he had thrown the world away and could therefore never admit to having made a mistake. But the cynic would be quite wrong.

To try and discover something about the woman who inspired such a deep and lasting love, and the man who lavished it upon her, is the purpose of this book.

*When Cecil Beaton visited Wallis at Cumberland Terrace in 1936 with proofs of her photographs, the King asked for prints of them all.*
*'Won't that be rather a Wallis Collection, Sir?' quipped Beaton. This portrait of Wallis was photographed by Beaton in 1934.*

# I

# A Young Lady
# from Baltimore

I was born an American, I will live an American,
I shall die an American.

*Daniel Webster*

B essie Wallis Warfield was born on 19 June 1896 in a summer
holiday cottage at Blue Ridge Summit in Pennsylvania, but
this was purest chance; the birth was a little premature and
the parents had gone to Blue Ridge Summit because the baby's
father was in delicate health and wanted to escape the heat of his
native Baltimore, where it had been planned that the child should
be born in the family house.

The Warfield family came to America in 1662, and Wallis was
descended from Governor Edwin Warfield of Maryland. They
were long-established and well-regarded in Baltimore. Her mother
was a Montague from Virginia; a relation of hers was Governor
of Virginia from 1902 to 1906. The Montagues were famous for
their good looks and their sharp tongues. In her memoirs the
Duchess of Windsor repeats some of her mother's wise cracks;
they do not strike the reader as particularly witty, but they evidently
seemed so at the time. 'Oh, the Montagueity of it!' exclaimed
people in the know when Wallis herself made an amusing remark.

All four grandparents had supported the Confederate cause in the
Civil War thirty years before; they were pro-British and anti-
Yankee. They were proud of the fact that Wallis's Warfield grand-
father had been arrested 'by Mr Lincoln's men'. He had died before
Wallis was born, but her grandmother had a hatred of Yankees
that would have startled even Jefferson Davis, and never allowed a
Northerner into her house. 'Never marry a Yankee,' she used to
say.

When Wallis (she dropped the Bessie as a small child, saying it
was the name of so many cows) was a few months old her father
died at the age of twenty-seven and her mother was left penniless.
The Warfields were not enormously rich but they were rich enough;

they supported the widow and orphan. Wallis had a happy child-hood; she adored her very pretty mother, who sent her to a fashionable day school in Baltimore. They lived for some years with her grandmother Warfield, who was kind but strict, and Wallis spent her holidays at the country-houses and farms of her uncles. The chief benefactor was her bachelor uncle, Solomon, a successful banker and President of the Continental Trust Company, whose office was known as Solomon's Temple. He paid the school fees and other bills until Mrs Warfield married again; her new husband, Mr J. F. Rasin, was fairly rich and like the Warfields and the Montagues, his family was prominent in politics. Wallis's mother was well-known for her delicious food, and with Mr Rasin she gave delightful dinner parties in Baltimore.

Wallis was now sent to a boarding school, Oldfields, which had the motto: 'Gentleness and Courtesy are Expected of the Girls at all Times.' The motto was pasted on the door of every room so that it should never be forgotten, and even the basket-ball teams were called Gentleness and Courtesy. Many years later, writing in her memoirs of this emphasis on good manners at Oldfields, Wallis said she found it preferable to the modern way which led to the 'uninhibited' behaviour of young people.

Wallis was good at games and good at lessons. She made lifelong friendships at Oldfields and seems to have been perfectly happy there. The head-mistress, Miss Nan McCulloh, was old-fashioned and strict. As was the custom in those days there was a great deal of learning by heart; 'Miss Nan' would not allow any girl to go home for the Christmas holidays until she could recite a chapter of the Bible, word-perfect. While she was at this school Wallis's step-father died in April 1913, and she and her mother became poor once again.

In 1914 she left Oldfields, signing her name and writing a message in the school book. Wallis wrote 'ALL IS LOVE'. The other girls' contributions were painfully silly; 'It's the little things that count', was one, another 'Long live English history.' Their cramped adolescent handwriting adds to the general impression of banality, whereas Wallis already had an adult, individual hand, her signature and her words springing from the page.

She made her début at a ball in Baltimore called the Bachelors' Cotillion on 24 December, wearing a white satin dress with white chiffon tunic bordered with pearls. Her taste in clothes never failed her. But her Uncle Sol, who had given a ball for her cousin, refused to give a coming-out party for Wallis. In Europe the Great War had begun. He put a notice in the newspapers saying he could not give a ball for his niece Wallis Warfield 'while men were being

*Left: Teackle Wallis Warfield, Wallis' father who died a few months after his daughter's birth*

*Below: The summer cottage at Blue Ridge Summit, Pennsylvania, where Wallis was born on 19 June 1896*

*Alice Montague Warfield with her daughter, Wallis, aged about six months*

*Left: Wallis with her grandmother, Mrs Warfield, a strict but kind lady with an undying hatred for anybody north of the Mason-Dixon line*

*Right: Wallis as a ten-year-old schoolgirl*

*Wallis' handwritten entry in her school yearbook, and, (below) Oldfields, the boarding school in Baltimore, to which Wallis was sent in 1912*

*Above: Wallis as a debutante. On Christmas Eve 1914 she made her début at the Bachelors' Cotillion, but the outbreak of the Great War in Europe had put paid to her hopes for a coming-out dance of her own*

*Right: Wallis aged nineteen. In 1915 her grandmother died and Wallis was sent to Florida to stay with her cousin Corinne Mustin. While staying with Corinne she met the man destined to become her first husband, Win Spencer*

slaughtered and their families left destitute in the appalling catastrophe now devastating Europe'. Eighteen months later catastrophe struck Wallis herself, though it did not seem so to her at the time.

Although the usual festivities were somewhat curtailed by the distant war, Wallis seems to have had what all through her life she used to call 'a good time'. She and the other members of Baltimore's *jeunesse dorée* had dances and parties in the evenings, and she spent the mornings in endless telephone conversations with her friends. Poor as they were, there was no thought of a job; just as in England at the same date girls like Wallis only had marriage to look forward to as a career. Not one of her class-mates at Oldfields had gone on to a university, let alone to a career.

In 1915 her grandmother, Mrs Warfield, died and the family was plunged into mourning. When some months later a cousin invited her to stay in Florida, Wallis's mother persuaded her to accept; she thought Wallis had mourned long enough, yet, according to the custom of those days, she could not rush about Baltimore having a good time. Her cousin Corinne was married to the commandant of the newly-established Pensacola Air Station, he was Captain Mustin of the United States Navy. Flying was in its infancy and airmen were all considered dashing heroes. The Pensacola airmen all hoped to get into the war in Europe, a wish that for most of them was soon to be granted.

The day after she arrived at Pensacola, Wallis wrote to her mother: 'I have just met the world's most fascinating aviator.' This was Lieutenant Earl Winfield Spencer Junior, United States Navy. They saw a great deal of each other, she was attracted to him and she made various excuses to stay on and on at Pensacola.

While she was there the foundations were laid for her life-long dread of flying. There was a 'crash gong' at the Air Station which often sounded. The wives and friends of airmen were not allowed to use the telephone when they heard the crash gong in case they interrupted an important call, and therefore everyone suffered horrible anxiety waiting to hear who had crashed and whether he was injured or even dead. Often the aeroplanes came down in the sea and the men were quickly picked up, but often too there were fatal accidents.

Win Spencer and Wallis saw each other every day and became more and more attached to one another. When he proposed she accepted him. A photograph of him taken at this time shows an alarming, rather brutal-looking man. His mouth is tightly shut, but he seems about to open it in order to utter some trenchant sarcasm. However, he is said to have had charm, and when during

*Right: 'The world's most fascinating aviator,' Lieutenant Earl Winfield Spencer*

*Below: Wallis, surrounded by her bridal attendants, at her marriage to Lieutenant Winfield Spencer on 12 November 1916 in Baltimore. Sitting on the left is Mary Kirk, Wallis' schoolfriend who was to marry Ernest Simpson after his divorce from Wallis*

his next leave Wallis introduced him to her mother, her Aunt Bessie Merryman and her Uncle Sol they gave a qualified blessing. Her mother warned Wallis that she might find it difficult to fit into the restricted life of a naval officer's wife, but none of them seems to have guessed how difficult, how impossible the man himself would prove to be. Wallis was in love, and she also knew that her marriage would relieve her mother of the burden of supporting her.

The young couple went to stay with the Spencers in a suburb of Chicago. Mrs Spencer was English. They welcomed Wallis and wished her and Win all possible happiness, but they could not help financially, and it was clearly understood that Win's pay was all that the couple would have to live on, which did not worry Wallis in the slightest. She was perfectly accustomed to making do with very little.

She was twenty when in November 1916 she and Win Spencer were married at Christ Church, Baltimore; the church where she had been confirmed a few years before was now filled with lilies and white chrysanthemums. She had six bridesmaids dressed in orchid-coloured *bouffant* gowns with blue velvet sashes; the ushers were in naval uniform. Wallis herself wore white panne velvet over a petticoat of heirloom lace, and a tulle veil with a coronet of orange blossom. Her uncle gave her away. When, at the reception, she 'threw her bouquet' it was caught by Mary Kirk, her best friend from Oldfield days, and shortly afterwards Mary married Captain Jacques Raffray, a Frenchman who came to the United States as liaison officer after America declared war.

During their short honeymoon Wallis and Win went to an hotel at White Sulphur Springs, West Virginia. She was looking out of the window at the garden when she heard an angry exclamation from Win. He had seen a printed notice under the glass of the dressing table which announced that West Virginia was a dry state and therefore no alcoholic drinks could be sold.

'We certainly can't stay here,' said Win, but he opened his box and produced a bottle of gin from among the shirts and socks. Wallis at the age of twenty had never yet tasted alcohol at all except for a glass of champagne at Christmas. At her mother's dinner parties no wine was given with the delicious food; there were 'assorted liquors' on a tray to be drunk before or after eating, which in many American houses is still the custom to this day. She soon discovered that Win drank far too much, and that when he had done so he became aggressive, rude and even violent. Wallis was in for a difficult time.

## II
# Navy Wife

Keep up appearances; there lies the test;
The world will give thee credit for the rest.

*Charles Churchill*

When they returned to the Air Station at Pensacola Wallis's cousin Corinne was on the platform to greet them. She ran along beside the train and called 'Hi, Skinny!' her name for the new Mrs Spencer. At the seaplane base, no longer a visitor but a Navy wife, Wallis settled into a bungalow, one of a row all alike. It had a living room, three bedrooms and two bathrooms; she put up chintz curtains, painted the furniture white and got a cook and a maid for thirty-two dollars a month. In the evenings she and the other officers' wives took turns to give little dinner parties and then they played poker. The pilots were forbidden to drink for twenty-four hours before flying, but at week-ends they celebrated. On Saturday nights they went to the local hotel and danced till dawn. Win was apt to do embarrassing imitations of vaudeville stars, dancing about in front of the band, but this was harmless enough.

During the week Wallis dreaded the crash gong more than ever. Once it sounded for Win, but he had come down in the sea and was rescued by the station launch. Now that war was near the number of recruits increased, and Win was kept very busy training them. On 6 April 1917 Congress declared war on the Central Powers. Win was promoted, and sent to Squantum, Massachusetts, near Boston, to take command of a new naval air station. He was bitterly disappointed; he had hoped to be sent to France for combat flying. 'Squantum! What a place to fight a war!' he said, and he decided to get away from his new job as soon as possible and go overseas. He was so successful at creating the Naval Air Base that he was ordered to California to organize a naval air station on North Island. This new assignment almost broke his heart; to be sent west, rather than east to the war, was bitter indeed.

San Diego, where he and Wallis were now to live, was then a

small semi-tropical town with Spanish bungalows set among palm trees and hibiscus. Win was working from dawn to dusk. Wallis began to do her own cooking, with the help of Fannie Farmer's *Boston Cooking School Book*, one of her wedding presents. Before her first dinner party she was so nervous that Win persuaded her to drink a cocktail. 'One for the cook,' he said, 'a sovereign receipt.' All nervousness banished by a double martini, Wallis produced a perfect dinner.

Win Spencer and his instructors had created a model air station, but the Armistice in 1918 found him deeply dissatisfied with his lot. There was now no hope for him of flying in combat. He became moody and difficult and he began to drink heavily. He made several enemies in the higher echelons of the Navy, and there seemed to Wallis to be less and less scope for his talents. She would have liked him to go into business in commercial aviation, but Win loved the Navy, and she resigned herself to the gypsy wanderings of a Service wife. Although she made many friends in California things were not easy between her and her husband, and when he was temporarily ordered back to Pensacola she was pleased, imagining that in new surroundings they could make a fresh start.

Spencer's next assignment was to the Navy Bureau of Aeronautics in Washington. It turned out to be the very worst thing that could have happened. He loved flying, and his new job consisted entirely of paper work, drafting reports and sitting in an office. He took to the bottle, and he was not a quiet drinker. They were living in a service flat in the Hotel Brighton, the walls were thin and Wallis realized that the wretchedness of their life together was known to their friends.

Then one Sunday afternoon Win locked her in the bathroom. Hours went by, evening came and Wallis longed to call for help but was too proud to do so. Finally she heard the key turn in the lock, but at first she dared not try to open the door. By the time she did so Win was in bed and asleep. She spent the night on a sofa, and when he had gone to the office next day she went to see her mother who was living in the city in Connecticut Avenue.

Wallis had decided to leave her husband and get a divorce. Not only had her own life become impossible, she also felt she made things worse for Win. He vented his furious frustrations upon her, and she thought that by removing herself she might be helping him. When she told her mother of her resolve there was a tremendous scene. No Montague had ever been divorced, said her mother, and such a thing was unthinkable. Her Aunt Bessie said the same; so divorce was out of the question. In any case, who would support her? Not her Uncle Sol. The Warfields were every bit as uncompromisingly strait-laced about divorce as the Montagues. When Wallis described the misery of her life with Win her mother relented a little. A separation was considered infinitely less scandalous. To Wallis this seemed not only hypocritical but wrong, since neither Win nor she could re-make life so long as they were bound together.

Wallis now had to face Uncle Sol; she went to Baltimore and bearded him in his Temple. His reaction was fierce. 'I won't let you bring this disgrace upon us!' he said, and he told her that ever since 1662, which was as far back as their records went, no Warfield had ever been divorced. He urged her to become reconciled to Win and she returned to Washington. It was clear to her that on both sides of her family the thought uppermost in their minds was: 'What will people say?' Nothing mattered very much but that; it was the powerful tyranny of public opinion which governed them.

A fortnight later she definitely made up her mind to leave Win. He behaved rather well. 'Wallis', he said, 'I've had this coming to me. If you ever change your mind I'll still be around.' She asked her mother if she might stay with her. 'You are absolutely sure that this is what you really want?' said her mother. 'If I've never been sure of anything before, I'm sure about this', was the reply. Wallis moved to her mother's flat and she wrote to Uncle Sol. He answered that any divorce action she might take must be entirely from her own resources; no help of any description would come from him.

Although Wallis was sometimes rather lonely in Washington she nevertheless managed to have quite a good time. There were plenty of parties and many of her friends were foreign diplomats. The one she liked best was Don Felipe Espil, first secretary of the Argentine Embassy. He was a good-looking man of thirty-five, and Wallis found him most attractive, but there could be no more than friendship between them since he was a Catholic diplomat representing a Catholic country. However, she makes it abundantly plain in her memoirs that but for this insurmountable obstacle she might have considered marrying him. This worried her mother, for Wallis was not divorced. In order to be more independent, she moved from her mother's flat and shared a little house in Georgetown, the prettiest part of Washington, with another 'navy wife'.

Luncheons given by *les soixante gourmets* were a highlight, and probably for the first time she realized what French cooking could be. The sixty gourmets met once a week, each of them bringing a lady guest. Years later she looked back on these occasions with undiminished pleasure. Anyone who knows Washington and its

*Above left: Wallis as a young naval wife in Coronado, California*

*Above: Don Felipe Espil, first secretary of the Argentine Embassy, who fascinated Wallis in Washington after her first estrangement from Win Spencer*

*Left: Wallis in 1928*

restaurants will appreciate how clever the sixty gourmets must have been to induce the cooks at the Hotel Hamilton, where the luncheons took place, to perform so brilliantly.

Wallis was popular. Lord Colyton, at that time Third Secretary at the British Embassy, writes: 'I knew her quite well in those days, and although we were not close friends, I was very fond of her.'*

When her cousin Corinne Mustin, now a widow, invited her to go to Paris she accepted with joy. She went to New York to ask Uncle Sol for money for the journey. She had never before seen his New York flat, and was amused to discover that the walls were papered with photographs of actresses and singers. Uncle Sol had all the traditional obsession with the stage of a typical puritan. After objecting to her plan of going to Paris with Corinne he pressed some bank notes into her hand and when she looked at them in the taxi leaving his flat she counted five new hundred-dollar bills.

Wallis and Corinne sailed to Europe in a small boat on a rough sea. When they got to Paris they quickly, through friends and the friends of friends, began to have a good time. When a lawyer was consulted about divorce, however, it turned out to be far more expensive than Wallis could afford; he asked several thousand dollars. All this time Win continued to write to her, and he now told her that he had been posted to the Far East. He begged her to join him in China, she could board a naval transport and go there at government expense. Perhaps because there was no practical alternative, perhaps because she was lonely, perhaps because the idea of visiting China appealed to her, Wallis decided to go, and thus give her marriage one more chance of success.

Back in Washington, Wallis's mother was surprised though gratified to hear she was going to join Win Spencer. The Navy Department made the arrangements, and on 17 July 1924 she boarded the *USS Chaumont*, bound for the Philippines, a slow voyage of six weeks. There she took the *Empress of Canada* to Hong Kong. She found Win looking fit and well, and at first everything was rosy. Before long, however, he started drinking again. 'I can't explain it. It's just me,' he told her. 'Something lets go—like the control cables of a plane.' Although when she became ill with a kidney complaint he nursed her with great kindness, they were soon back to square one. He drank, he was moody, jealous and impossible. She decided it was a hopeless case and that she would try to get a divorce at the United States Court for China in Shanghai. Win saw her off: 'Pensacola, Boston, Coronado, Washington and now Hong Kong' he said. 'We've come a long way, only to lose what we began with.'

*Letter to the author.

This was the end of Wallis's first marriage, which had lasted on and off for eight years. She was now twenty-eight and her character was formed. She was independent but not tough, rather easily hurt with a rare capacity for making friends wherever she went. She was intelligent and quick, amusing, good company, an addition to any party with her high-spirited gaiety. Without being either particularly beautiful or pretty she was always noticed for her perfect figure and elegant clothes. She loved and appreciated good food, but ate so little that she remained triumphantly thin at a time when slenderness was all-important in fashion. Her talent was for people; witty herself, she had the capacity to draw the best out of others, making even the dull feel quite pleased with themselves. This rare gift developed as the years went by.

*Four generations of British monarchy at the christening of Prince Edward in 1894. Queen Victoria; her son, the future Edward VII; her grandson, the Duke of York, the future George V; and in her arms the future Edward VIII*

# III

# *The Little Prince*

Love is not changed by Death,
And nothing is lost and all in the end is harvest.

*Edith Sitwell*

Far from easy-going if puritan Baltimore, arranged marriages were still the rule in the royal families of nineteenth-century Europe; they were rather cold-blooded affairs, even though they often worked quite well. The marriage arranged between Prince George of Wales, Duke of York, and Princess May of Teck seemed to many people more than usually cold-blooded.

Queen Victoria was looking for a girl who would be a suitable Queen consort to marry Prince Albert Victor, Duke of Clarence, the Prince of Wales's eldest son. She thought Princess May of Teck might be the best possible choice, and therefore commanded the Princess and her brother Prince Adolphus to go to her at Balmoral.

Princess May's mother, the popular and immensely fat Mary Adelaide, Duchess of Teck, was Queen Victoria's cousin. She was enchanted at this invitation to Balmoral, for she guessed its reason. That her daughter should marry the heir to the throne had always been her wildest ambition. Various German princelings who might have been suitors for Princess May's hand were prevented from proposing to her because of a 'stain' – the Duke of Teck's morganatic birth. While the Duchess was a Royal Highness, the Duke of Teck and Princess May were merely Serene Highnesses, a disadvantage swept to one side by Queen Victoria.

The Duke of Clarence, always called Eddy in the family, was volatile, indolent and pleasure-loving. In contrast to Princess May, and to his father the Prince of Wales, (later Edward VII), he had received only a very sketchy education. He had fallen in love with Princess Hélène of Orléans and she with him, but she was a Roman Catholic and neither her parents nor Prince Eddy's could allow them to marry, although at one juncture Prince Eddy offered to renounce his succession to the throne in favour of his brother

Prince George. This difficulty about Princess Hélène having been surmounted, Prince Eddy fell in love again – twice in as many months. His parents and his grandmother were anxious for the capricious young man, and Queen Victoria thought Princess May might be a steadying influence and set about getting to know her.

The stay at Balmoral lasted ten days. 'We have seen a great deal of May and Dolly Teck during their ten days visit here and I cannot say enough good of them. May is a particularly nice girl, so quiet and yet cheerful and so carefully brought up and so sensible. She is grown very pretty,' wrote Queen Victoria to her daughter the Empress Frederick. The Empress was unimpressed. 'I am so glad to hear you are pleased with May and Dolly Teck. I wonder whether Eddy will ever marry May ... Some people said there was not much in May – that she was a little *oberflächlich* [superficial]' she wrote.

Queen Victoria replied: 'I think and hope that Eddy will try and marry her ... she is the reverse of *oberflächlich*', and she wrote to the young Tecks' mother: 'I never had an opportunity before of knowing May well or Dolly either ... they are so well brought up and have such good manners which in the present day is not *too* frequent. May is a dear, charming girl.'

The Duke and Duchess of Teck were overjoyed, and the prospective bridegroom's father the Prince of Wales seemed to think Prince Eddy would come up to scratch; he wrote to the Queen: 'You may I think make your mind quite easy about Eddy and that he has made up his mind to propose to May but we thought it best *de ne pas brusquer les choses* as she is coming to us with her parents after Xmas to Sandringham.'

However, to the surprise of all, Prince Eddy proposed that very evening, 3 December 1891. At a country-house party he took Princess May into his hostess's boudoir and asked her to marry him. Everyone was delighted, the Tecks, Queen Victoria, the Prince and Princess of Wales, and 'the country'. Princess May, shy but happy, was cheered at St Pancras Station on her way home.

Man proposes, Fate disposes. While Princess May and her parents were staying at Sandringham early in the New Year 1892, Prince Eddy became ill with influenza. He was not robust. He developed inflammation of the lungs and pneumonia; many doctors were sent for. While raging fever made him delirious Prince Eddy's family crowded into his little bedroom; his mother sat at his bedside holding his hand and fanning his brow. Princess May shared a chair with 'Harry', Princess Maud of Wales. Early on 14 January he died.

There is no doubt that Prince Eddy was deeply mourned by

everyone who knew him. '*Il était si bon!*' as his former love Princess Hélène said to Queen Victoria. *Bon* he was and charming, but with his flaccid, easily-influenced nature he might not have made the very best of kings even with sensible Princess May to support him. At the time, however, people were stunned by the tragedy of his sudden death. Letters and telegrams flew to Sandringham from all over Europe. 'This is an overwhelming misfortune . . . The poor Parents it is *too dreadful* for them to think of! and the poor young Bride!' wrote Queen Victoria. A popular ballad composed for the occasion had the refrain:

> A nation wrapped in mourning
> Shed bitter tears today
> For the noble Duke of Clarence
> And fair young Princess May.

While Prince Eddy was dying the excitable and overwrought Duke of Teck, to the embarrassment of his family, was heard to say over and over again: '*It must be a Tsarevitch.*' The Princess of Wales had a sister, Princess Dagmar, who had been betrothed to the Tsarevitch Nicholas, heir to the throne of Russia. Nicholas had died and the following year Princess Dagmar married his brother Alexander. This pattern was now to be repeated in England.

Soon after the death of the Duke of Clarence, Queen Victoria made his brother Prince George, the new heir presumptive, Duke of York. His marriage now became a matter of urgent concern to the royal family. Queen Victoria was fond of him and thought him 'so nice, sensible and truly right-minded', but none of the Wales children was very strong,* and Prince George had been seriously ill with typhoid fever. It was essential that he marry without delay. One or two cousins were considered, but Queen Victoria still hoped that Princess May would be the future Queen consort of England.

In May 1893 the Duke of York proposed. A girl like Princess May, imbued as she was with reverence for the Throne, with her strong sense of duty, and conscious of her mother's fond ambition to see her on the way to becoming Queen consort of England, could never have refused such an offer even had she felt less than enthusiastic about her cousin the Duke of York. Fortunately she liked him, and the tragedy of Prince Eddy's death had linked them

---

*The Queen had described them to her daughter, then Crown Princess of Prussia: 'they are such miserable, puny little children, each weaker than the preceding one, that it is quite a misfortune. I can't tell you how these poor, frail little fairies distress me . . . darling Papa [the Prince Consort] would have been in perfect despair.' Queen Victoria was a keen amateur geneticist, like the Prince Consort who had often wished for an infusion of strong dark blood into the royal family. Princess May was fair and blue-eyed, but there was dark Hungarian blood in the Duke of Teck.

together in a common sorrow. It may have been duty, it may have been something akin to love; nobody will ever know and it is more than possible that the Princess hardly knew herself. She accepted without demur and they were married in July. The newspapers, determined upon a romance, pretended that Princess May had been 'in love' with Prince George all along. However that may be, their letters to one another during their engagement speak of love; after they married they became an ideal couple and a pattern of domestic behaviour for the rest of their lives. Not quite everyone was pleased at the news of the betrothal. 'One can only think of the engagement with very mixed feelings,' wrote the Empress Frederick to her daughter.

The honeymoon was spent at York Cottage, a little house near Sandringham which has been variously described as 'a glum little villa' and 'an ornate hutch'. Moreover, Prince George had not waited for his bride to choose the furnishings but had summoned 'Maple's man' with dire results for the interior. Small and inconvenient as it undoubtedly was, however, York Cottage was loved by the Duke of York. He had the royal predilection for what was 'cosy' and 'snug'.

Queen Victoria did not approve of the choice of venue for the honeymoon; everything at Sandringham must have reminded the newly wedded pair of the tragedy they had lived through together eighteen months before. 'The young couple go to Sandringham to the Cottage after the Wedding which I regret and think rather *unlucky* and sad,' she wrote to her eldest daughter.

Eleven months later, on 23 June 1894, their eldest son, the future Duke of Windsor, was born at White Lodge, Richmond Park, the Tecks' house. The Duke of York noted in his diary: 'At 10 a sweet little boy was born. Mr Asquith [the Home Secretary] came to see him.' The child was christened Edward Albert Christian George Andrew Patrick David. Queen Victoria, as usual, wanted Albert to be the first name, but the Yorks had determined to call him Edward 'after darling Eddy'. The Queen wrote: 'You write as if *Edward* was the real name of dear Eddy ... while it was Albert Victor which Papa again and again said was his *real* official appellation.' Queen Victoria was destined to be frustrated in her ardent desire that the hallowed name of Albert should be the name of future kings of England. Although Edward VII and George VI were both called Albert and known in the family as Bertie, they changed the name when they came to the throne.*

*The author asked the Duke of Windsor how 'Bertie' was pronounced in the royal family; was it 'Bartie' like the surname or 'Bertie' to rhyme with Gertie? He thought for a moment and then said: 'Neither, it was "Bairty". *Sehr deutsch*!' But this obviously only applied to his grandfather.

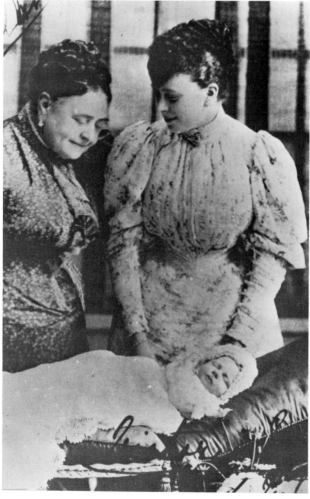

*Above: York Cottage,
Sandringham, the
honeymoon choice and
subsequent family home
of the Duke and Duchess
of York. Originally used
as the Bachelors' Cottage
for Sandringham, it was
given to the Duke by his
father as a wedding
present. Although the
Duke loved it, Sir Harold
Nicolson was later to
describe it as: 'a glum
little villa, encompassed
by thickets of laurel and
rhododendron . . .
separated by an abrupt
line of lawn from a pond,
at the edge of which a
leaden pelican gazes in
dejection.'*

*Left: On 23 June 1894
'a sweet little boy' was
born to the Duke and
Duchess of York at
White Lodge, Richmond.
The infant Prince
Edward, admired by his
mother, Princess May,
and his grandmother
Princess Mary, Duchess
of Teck*

A christening photograph was taken of Queen Victoria holding 'the dear fine baby' on her lap with her son Bertie and grandson Georgie standing behind her – four generations, all four of them monarchs. Amid the rejoicing over the birth the Scotch Socialist, Keir Hardie, made a speech in the House of Commons: 'From his childhood this boy will be surrounded by sycophants and flatterers by the score, and will be taught to believe himself of a superior creation. A line will be drawn between him and the people he might be called to rule over. In due course . . . he will be sent on a tour round the world, and probably rumours of a morganatic marriage will follow, and the end of it will be that the country will be called upon to pay the bill.' Quoting this sour pronouncement more than half a century later the Duke of Windsor described it as 'uncannily clairvoyant'.

Five more children were born to the Duke and Duchess of York, but the eldest, known to the public as Prince Edward and called David in the family, was the one upon whom attention was focussed. The children were brought up in the 'ornate hutch', York Cottage. Their parents were often in London or overseas on official duty, but even when they were at home the Duchess of York saw very little of her children. The Duke's aunt, the Empress Frederick, wrote of her: 'May . . . does not seem to have the passionate tenderness for her little ones which seems so natural to me. She has something very cold and stiff . . . I like her very much and she and Georgie seem so happy and contented together . . . I do *not* think her clever but', she added more kindly, 'I should say she would never do or say a foolish thing'. Perhaps because their own mothers, Queen Alexandra and the Duchess of Teck, were almost exaggeratedly gushing, the Yorks were very reserved and the Duchess of York never got near to having an intimate or loving relationship with her eldest son. As was usual at that time in households with a Nanny and nursery maids, family life consisted only of a visit by the children to their parents after tea. What was unusual was that the nurse gave Prince Edward's arm a good pinch just as she brought him into the drawing room, so that he should cry and scream and be quickly removed. His mother took some time to discover the reason for this unattractive behaviour and dismiss the nurse, despite the fact that York Cottage was so small that when asked where the servants slept the Duke of York said he supposed it must be in the trees. Lady Airlie, who was often at York Cottage as lady-in-waiting, had a bedroom little bigger than a cupboard. She describes the nurseries as 'dark and depressing'. According to her the Duchess of York was 'tragically inhibited with her children'.

*Prince Edward (far left) standing to attention with his brothers, Prince Albert (the future George VI), Prince Henry, and his sister, Princess Mary*

*Two photographs from the Prince's own albums: (left) with his brother Bertie in 1912;
and in naval uniform on the bridge of a warship in 1913 (above)*

In fairness to the future Queen Mary it must be said that she made a better job of her relationship with Prince Edward than the Empress Frederick did with Kaiser William II, who detested his mother and behaved very unkindly to her as soon as he was able.

Unlike Prince Albert, who tried to have the future Edward VII stuffed with knowledge (he tried in vain, but the attempt was laudable) the Duke of York gave his sons a minimum of 'book learning'. The York children were educated by a tutor at the Cottage until the boys could go into the Navy. The Duke of York was convinced that the Navy would teach his sons all that they needed to know.

Lack of affection is something for which no parents can be blamed. If it is not in them it can hardly be simulated. Not to have given a future King even a chance of learning may seem a grave error; by the time Prince Edward went to Oxford he had fallen far behind his contemporaries. On the other hand it is doubtful whether whatever opportunities had been put in his way the result would have been very different.

Light relief from the drear of the Cottage was provided during their grandparents' lifetime, or rather until their grandfather Edward VII died, by visits to the Big House when the King and Queen were in residence. The children were welcomed and made much of by their grandparents and the cheerful lords and pretty ladies of the entourage. Even then the Duke of York did his best to make them miserable on their return to York Cottage, where he awaited them, watch in hand, and scolded them for being late. These glimpses of fun and luxury were doubtless an important ingredient in the upbringing of the Prince. He realized that boredom and scoldings were not all that life contained, even for princes. The duties of a constitutional monarch are often less than exhilarating, and in order to be able to perform them with the required enthusiasm a certain amount of amusement during spare time is indispensable. King George V's favourite relaxation was shooting; he was a first-class shot and he also liked sailing. His other hobby was philately; in London he spent hours 'playing with his stamps'.*

In the House of Hanover there was a long and almost unbroken tradition of strong dislike of the heir to the throne by the monarch all through the eighteenth and nineteenth centuries. Queen Victoria could not stand the future Edward VII until he was quite old, and he certainly gave cause for complaint on more than one occasion. When George V came to the throne his eldest son, now to be Prince of Wales, was sixteen. He was accustomed to his father's bullying; to the natural dislike that a very conventional

*One of his courtiers in conversation with the author.

man often feels for an adolescent was added in this case an equally natural grain of jealousy of the physical beauty and winning manners of the Prince. As the eldest of the family, Prince Edward had acted as lightning conductor, and his martinet of a father did not scold the other children quite so much. Thinking back to another fierce father of a charming son, King Frederick William of Prussia, the future Frederick the Great in some ways had an easier time of it as a child than Prince Edward, because his mother and sister were his allies and except when the King was actually present they could all laugh together. It is doubtful whether Prince Edward's next brother and his sister, Prince Bertie and Princess Mary, would have found much humour in their situation, and it is quite certain that Queen Mary would not for one instant have countenanced jokes about her husband.

# IV

# Prince of Wales

Courts and camps are the only places
to learn the world in.

*Lord Chesterfield*

W hen he came to the throne in 1910, George V made Prince
Edward Prince of Wales, and this was to be his name for
the next twenty-five years. It was Lloyd George who
devised what the Prince thought was a rather absurd pseudo-
medieval ceremony at Caernarvon Castle, where the King was to
present the Prince to the Welsh people. For this much-publicized
occasion he was obliged to wear fancy dress, which he minded
dreadfully, knowing all too well what his fellow naval cadets
would think about his get-up. The King was adamant, but this time
Queen Mary showed sympathy for her son. She told him that
princes often had to do silly things, but that people quite understood it was not their fault. He put on the hated clothes and went
through with it. 'It was a most picturesque and beautiful ceremony,' wrote Queen Mary, 'and very well arranged. David looked
charming in his purple and miniver cloak and gold circlet and did
his part very well. The heat was awful.'

The Prince had been coached by Lloyd George, and taught to
say a few words in Welsh, including the sentence: 'All Wales is a
sea of song.' During these lessons the two of them became great
friends; Lloyd George was among the Prince's most faithful
admirers and the admiration was mutual. The same thing applied
to Winston Churchill, who as Home Secretary was also at Caernarvon Castle.

The Prince had the good looks, though on a smaller scale, of the
Queen's brother, Prince Dolly, whose golden beauty she had much
admired in her youth. Yet Queen Mary was anxious about her son,
whose tastes were so unlike her own, who seemed to love what she
was later to call 'rushing about', an activity disliked by her. She
confided her worries to Lord Esher, walking by the river at Balmoral. They discussed 'every conceivable detail of the Prince of

Wales's character, education, temptations, etc.' he wrote, and he promised to send her some notes on *'l'éducation d'un prince'*.

King George now removed the Prince of Wales from Dartmouth and sent him to France to learn the language. He never managed much French, but his German was fluent, for he had cousins in so many of the German courts with whom he stayed the following year. It was Mr Hansell, tutor to the royal children, who persuaded the King that the Prince ought to go to Oxford. The King finally consented and he was sent to Magdalen. Mr Hansell went too. Queen Mary's Aunt Augusta, the Grand Duchess of Mecklenburg-Strelitz, wrote to her niece: 'Why is he to be an undergraduate? Surely this cannot be true! it is too democratic; and why? And why does his Tutor *again* accompany him?' Why indeed. It may have seemed unduly democratic to the Grand Duchess, but not only Mr Hansell went to Oxford with the Prince. His valet went too, as well as an equerry, Major Cadogan. For once an equerry justified his name and Major Cadogan taught him to ride; it was through him that for years fox-hunting became the Prince's favourite sport. There was not very much 'book learning', but the Prince made a number of new friends, and, as he said himself: 'Ever since I can remember, it has been from people rather than from text-books that I have got my education.'

In the autumn of 1913, during his second year at Oxford, the Prince was summoned to Windsor for the visit of the Archduke Franz Ferdinand, heir presumptive to the Austro-Hungarian Imperial throne, and of his morganatic wife, the Duchess of Hohenberg. The Archduke was a noted shot and there was a monster bag at the Windsor shoot. This was only seven months before the 'elegant couple', as the Prince later described them, were murdered at Sarajevo. The Archduke had invited George V to shoot with him in the autumn of 1914; another guest was to have been the German Emperor, William II, known in England as the Kaiser. When the date of the shooting party came round, the Archduke was dead and his prospective guests were at war.

The Prince of Wales did not much care for royal visits to his parents which he was obliged to attend. Early in 1914 the Danish King and Queen came and there was a banquet. 'I took in Granny,' he wrote. 'Then we stood about in the picture gallery till 11.15 talking to the guests. What rot and a waste of time, money and energy all these State visits are! This is my only remark on all this unreal show and ceremony!'

That summer the Prince was twenty; during the London season he went to a ball nearly every night. At first he was shy, but after a while: 'I have now become fond of dancing and love

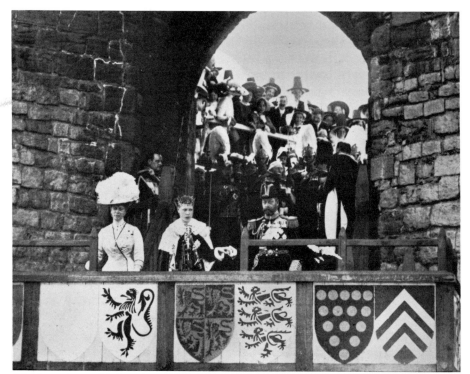

*The investiture of Edward as Prince of Wales in Caernarvon Castle in 1911. For the ceremony the Prince wore white satin breeches and a mantle and surcoat of purple velvet edged with ermine, which he, a young naval cadet, called 'preposterous rig'. The King is shown presenting his son to the people of Wales*

*In April 1912 the Prince was sent to France to learn the language: the experiment was not very successful, for he was never to be fluent in French*

*A photograph from the Prince's album in the first year of the Great War*

going out! ... I've had no more than eight hours sleep in the last seventy-two hours.' He was attached to the 1st Life Guards and had to report at the barracks early each morning.

Ever since the fatal 28 June when Franz Ferdinand and his wife were assassinated threats and counter-threats had reverberated all over the Continent, but in London life went on just as usual. Towards the end of July the full international implications of what the Prince was later to describe as 'this villainous act' became apparent. Prince Henry of Prussia called at Buckingham Palace to say goodbye to his first cousin the King. 'We were coming out of church when he arrived' wrote the Prince. 'Uncle Henry and I shook hands warmly. I had happy memories of my stay at Hemmelmark the year before, and I felt that his Anglophile sentiments made him dread the awful possibility of war between our two countries as much as we did. I never saw him again.'

When war was declared on 4 August there was an explosion of public enthusiasm and rejoicing; crowds gathered outside Buckingham Palace and the King and Queen had to go on the balcony and be vociferously acclaimed. The general view, even among those who might have known better, was that the fighting would be over by Christmas. With the hindsight of two great wars lasting four and six years this may seem more absurdly optimistic than it did in 1914. When France and Germany had fought in 1870 the war had been fairly quickly over. The French had then introduced three years' compulsory military service and their great army looked forward to a spectacular revenge. Nobody foresaw the holocaust of trench warfare, hundreds of thousands of men killed for a gain of a few square miles of mud. After witnessing the demonstration at the palace the Prince wrote: 'I was lulled to sleep by their fearful shindy at 1.30. The die is cast; may God protect the fleet!'

He asked the King for a commission in the Grenadiers. 'Dear Papa never hesitated a moment and immediately instructed Lord Stamfordham to notify this to the War Office,' he wrote. 'It was a happy moment for me, and now I am an officer in the Army and am going to do active service! I get away from this awful palace where I have had the worst weeks of my life!' But although he got away from the awful palace it was only to go to Warley Barracks in Essex. After hard training they were sent back to London and in mid-September the Battalion went to France. The Prince was left behind. 'It was a terrible blow to my pride,' he wrote later, 'the worst in my life'. Trying to conceal his bitterness he asked the King why this had to be, and was told: 'Lord Kitchener does not want you to be in France just now.' He bearded Kitchener at the

War Office. 'What does it matter if I am killed?' he said, 'I have four brothers.' Lord Kitchener said he could not risk the Prince being taken prisoner by the enemy.

In the long casualty lists the Prince of Wales found the names of many friends with whom he had trained only a few weeks before. Among them was his equerry Major Cadogan. 'I shan't have a friend left soon,' he wrote in his diary. Eventually he was sent overseas, though only to a staff appointment. He began to appeal to Lord Stamfordham, who had the ear of the King, to be allowed to go into the front line. 'Our poor 1st Battalion had seven officers killed and seven wounded. Ghastly.' he wrote to the old courtier in March 1915.

> Of course my position at such times as these four days becomes all the more painful and depressing when I know I am only to be a spectator. . . . There is no job I am qualified for but that of a regimental officer . . . though it is sad to have to say it, I have no *real* job except that of being P. of Wales . . . I am awfully sorry for inflicting you with all my small troubles, but you have always been and are so good and kind to me that I can't help it.

After September 1915 the Prince was appointed to the staff of Major-General (afterwards Field-Marshal) Lord Cavan, who commanded the Guards Division, and from then on he was often near the front line and saw much of the fighting. When his own driver was killed he received a letter from Lord Stamfordham saying that the King was content to leave the decision to Lord Cavan as to where and when he went to the front. 'But, Sir, you who are so thoughtful for others, will not, I feel *certain*, forget Lord Cavan and the heavy weight of responsibility resting upon him in his Command and remember that your safety, your Life, so precious to your Country, is *another* care which circumstances have devolved upon him. Make it as light for him as you can, Sir! To anyone of your nature it is hard, very hard, to be left behind when the others are at the danger points.' Lord Stamfordham wrote this just after his only son had been killed in action.

The Prince was present when the King visited the armies after the battle of Loos. In order that the troops might see him better, General Haig had lent him his own supposedly very quiet and crowd-trained charger. The King rode among the ranks, until one of the officers called for 'Three cheers for His Majesty the King'. At the loud and sudden shout the horse took fright, reared up and fell back on top of the King, who suffered a fractured pelvis, an agonizing accident.

Sent to Egypt in 1916 the Prince was taken to Khartoum where

*The Prince with his father, George V, in France 1915*

officers still talked of General 'Chinese' Gordon. He had seen Gordon's Bible at Windsor, the very one he had with him 'at the time he was run through by the spears of the maddened Fuzzy-Wuzzies on the steps of his Residency' as the Prince described it.

His war service brought him into contact with men of all kinds in a way that could hardly have happened in peace time. Back in France he still chafed: 'Oh! to be fighting with those grand fellows and not sitting back here doing so little as compared with them who are sacrificing their lives! There could be no finer death.' He was still on Lord Cavan's staff when there is a glimpse of him in Italy in the memoirs of Sir Colin Coote, who had a period with a French division on the Italian front. Coote heartily disliked the French divisional commander who, according to him, was 'a grumbling, foul-mouthed swine'. The Prince of Wales paid them a visit during which 'he could and did charm that French divisional staff into raptures. Even the General thawed, and later said: "After all, your nation can produce a civilized man," a remark absolutely typical of the brute.'

What did the 'grand fellows' in the Guards think of him? A confidential report sent in by Lord Cavan in March 1916 says:

As I had the honour of having HRH the Prince of Wales, KG, on my staff ... I beg to submit a report on HR Highness ... I have no hesitation in saying that HR Highness has endeared himself to every officer and man in the Guards Division – not only on account of his keenness and anxiety for their well-being but also on account of his high courageous spirit which chafes at the restraint that his high position enforces.

Nevertheless I have taken opportunities to show HR Highness as much as possible of life in the front trenches, and especially the battle of Loos ... and from what I have seen of him ... I can but regret that the services of so fearless an officer should not be available for ordinary duty with his regiment.

As a staff officer he was very quick at picking up instructions and was very particularly efficient at organizing any out-of-door work such as regulation of refilling points and making arrangements for the transfer of rations from lorry to supply wagons by cleanly and smart methods.

HRH always kept himself in the pink of condition truly setting an excellent example to other young officers.

For these reasons I should certainly have considered HRH worthy of 'mention in despatches' and I hope that his good service and excellent example may not be overlooked.

*Signed* Cavan, Lt General XIV Corps.

The war dragged on, first one side then the other gaining a slight advantage, until America was thrown into the scales so that virtually the whole world was fighting against the Central Powers. In November 1918 the Allies had won the war and an Armistice was signed. All over Europe thrones toppled, first in Russia and then in Germany, Austria and Hungary.

# V

# Divorce and Re-marriage

I looked at the dragon-pond,
   with its willow-coloured water
Just reflecting the sky's tinge,
And heard the five-score nightingales
   aimlessly singing.

*Ezra Pound*

Wallis arrived in Shanghai in 1924 knowing nobody, but a letter of introduction to a man she calls 'Robbie' (his real name was Harold Robinson) led to the good time she always had wherever she happened to be. The hope of getting a divorce from Win Spencer quickly faded, but she decided to stay on for a while. There were garden parties and racing and dancing; the hospitable foreign colony consisted mostly of English people. When one of the American Navy wives suggested going to Peking for a shopping expedition Wallis accepted; she had always wanted to see Peking. She knew that an old friend, Colonel Louis Little, commanded the US Legation Guard there. The American Consul at Tientsin warned her and her companion that to travel further was unsafe. A local war was being fought, and trains were constantly being raided by bandits. The other Navy wife decided to give up the idea of Peking when the Consul threatened to report to the Navy that in going there she had disregarded the advice of the US Government representative. 'My husband would never forgive me if I went against the Consul and something awful happened,' she said.

But Wallis, having come so far, took the train, and although it arrived eight hours late and had several times been boarded by bandits she was none the worse. Colonel Little, who had been told of her journey by the Tientsin Consul, was on the platform to meet her. He was visibly annoyed, but soon accepted the situation. Wallis stayed at the Grand Hôtel de Pékin. She intended to spend a couple of weeks sight-seeing and shopping, but she fell in with an old friend, Katherine Moore Bigelow, now married to Herman Rogers. This couple was destined to be important in Wallis's life. The Rogers invited her to stay with them at their house in the Tartar

City, a lovely old house in a garden hidden behind a high wall. Stipulating that she must be allowed to pay her way, Wallis accepted; so cheap was Peking in those days for Americans that she could easily afford it. She supplemented her allowance as a Navy wife by her winnings at poker.

Her visit to Peking was one of the happiest times of her life and she always looked back upon it with pleasure as a peaceful interlude. She was fond of Katherine and Herman Rogers, and they of her. She loved the beauty of her surroundings, her daily ride with her hosts in the glacis round the Legation quarter, and above all the week-ends they spent in a temple hired from the local priest. It was high up in the Western Hills; they motored to the foot hills and rode the rest of the way on donkeys. Herman Rogers was an intelligent, well-read man who had studied Chinese history and Chinese art. The foreign colony in Peking, diplomats and business men, provided gaiety, but her visit to China was not just the usual good time and she enjoyed it much more. It was in Peking that she made friends with Georges Sebastian, a Rumanian brought up in France. He was a man of taste and a perfectionist such as she was later to become herself, he was doubtless a great influence upon her. When he left Peking Sebastian went to Tunis, where in 1928 he built himself a beautiful house at Hammamet. He supervized the restoration of the Medina there, forbidding electric wires (and, later, television aerials) so that nothing should spoil the purity of the sky-line. Long afterwards, in the 1950s, it was to him that Wallis turned when she thought of building a house in Spain.

Many months went by before she could make up her mind to leave this idyllic existence and go back to America. On the voyage home she became ill. She was put ashore at Seattle and taken to hospital where she had an operation. When she had sufficiently recovered she took the train east; at Chicago, Win Spencer unexpectedly appeared and travelled with her to Washington. This rather touching reunion was their last; they never saw one another again.

Staying with her mother in Washington, Wallis now discovered that she could get a divorce for desertion if she lived for a year in Virginia. Different States had different divorce laws and all she had to do was establish residence; the rest was easy and not expensive. She lodged in an hotel at Warrenton and before long she became acquainted with Virginia's horsey set. She had intended to enrich her mind during lonely months at Warrenton and she had provided herself with plenty of books, but she was soon as much in demand as ever for dinners and parties. She sometimes

*Shanghai in the 1920s: (above) the Bund and the British Concession; (below) a
shopping street*

*The British Legation in Peking, with the minister's residence on the right, and (left) a temple on the Tartar Wall, Peking*

visited her mother, and often stayed with her old friend Mary Kirk, now Mme Raffray, who lived in Washington Square, New York.

Her great preoccupation at this time was deciding how to set about earning her living. She knew she had a talent for clothes which might be turned into money, and she entered a competition in a fashion magazine; the winner was to be taken onto the editorial staff. She was in New York staying with the Raffrays and she sat up all night polishing her essay. Weeks later she got a letter from the magazine rejecting her effort. Thus discouraged, she attempted to learn about the selling of tubular steel for a Pittsburgh business man whose wife was a friend of hers. 'Nobody else seems to be able to sell it. Maybe Wallis can,' said Mrs Schiller. After three weeks at Pittsburgh Wallis decided that tubular steel was not for her.

It was at this juncture that she started seeing a good deal of Ernest Simpson, whom she had met with the Raffrays. He, like Wallis, was in the process of getting divorced. When she went back to Warrenton he gave her an armful of books to take with her. In New York that time she visited a fortune-teller who told her she would have two more husbands and become 'a famous woman'.

In 1926 her mother, now aged fifty-six, married again, a Washington man, Charles Gordon Allen. The wedding was a small family affair, and a few weeks later Wallis's Cousin Lelia invited them all for a party at Wakefield Manor to celebrate the Fourth of July. Her mother wrote in the visitors' book: 'Here on the Fourth with my Third,' which was evidently considered one of her vintage wise cracks. A better one, dating from the same period, was the caption she wrote under a snapshot of herself sitting on Mr Allen's knee: 'Me on my last lap.'

During the summer of 1927 Wallis was taken to Europe by her Aunt Bessie. They visited Naples, Palermo and the Dalmatian coast, Monte Carlo, Avignon and Arles. Aunt Bessie returned to America while Wallis went to Lake Maggiore with friends. Back in Paris she read in the *Paris Herald* that her Uncle Sol had died. She sailed for home. Uncle Sol had left most of his fortune to charity, but Wallis received a small annuity.

In December 1927 she got her divorce from Win Spencer; Simpson was also free and he asked her to marry him. Ernest Simpson's father was English, and he was to take over the family's shipping business in England. Wallis asked him for time to think about his proposal. She sailed for Europe and spent the spring staying with Katherine and Herman Rogers, who were now living near Cannes in a villa called Lou Viei. While she was there she wrote to Ernest Simpson and told him she would marry him.

*Wallis' mother, Alice, who was twice widowed and married Charles Gordon Allen as her third husband in 1926*

It is hard to resist the thought that for the second time Wallis was marrying because there was nothing much else she could do. She had tried, and failed, to get a job. She had very little money and no home to go to. Simpson was not a particularly attractive man but he was a determined suitor. He was well-read, widely travelled, with courtly manners; and he was fairly rich. Above all, he admired Wallis, who was everything that he could never be, spontaneous, amusing, popular, high-spirited. They were married at Chelsea Registry Office; the bride wore a yellow dress and a blue coat she had bought in Paris. They motored through France in a yellow Lagonda. Ernest Simpson knew his way about. He spoke good French and in Paris he took her to little restaurants where they had delicious food. They did a lot of sight-seeing; Simpson according to Wallis was the *Guide Michelin*, *Baedeker* and an encyclopaedia rolled into one. She was pleased with their honeymoon.

Back in London they took a furnished house, 12 Upper Berkeley Street, for one year. Wallis had a butler, a cook, a housemaid and a chauffeur. Her sister-in-law, Mrs Kerr Smiley, introduced her to her friends. At Upper Berkeley Street Wallis's genius for 'house-keeping' first had real scope. She did her shopping herself and chose well. This was unheard of in the London of those days: the cook always bought the food, usually ordering it on the telephone so that the shops did the choosing. Like all Americans, Wallis thought English table manners odd; eating with knife and fork, and not waiting to begin until everyone had got their food, as is the custom in America.

The English seemed to Wallis very snobbish about titles and positively off their heads when it came to royalty. She could not get over the interest shown in the most trivial doings of the King and Queen. She thought this obsession was universal, while in fact it was a feature in those days of exactly the circle she had married into; with the middle-class Simpsons she experienced this particular snobbery at its most potent.

When, however, Wallis says in her memoirs: 'Queen Mary had only to change her coat to start a new style' she is obviously having a quiet laugh to herself, because Queen Mary never changed her coat. She adhered to the fashion of her youth and though everyone liked her iron-clad appearance, long skirts, frizzled hair, waisted dresses and toques made of massed pansies, nobody would have dreamed of copying them, when the fashion was for the short, shapeless chiffon shift, shingled hair and the *cloche* hat.

The winter of 1928 was exceptionally cold and there were terrible London pea-soup fogs, now a thing of the past. The fogs

*In 1928 Wallis married Ernest Simpson and they settled in London at 12 Upper Berkeley Street*

were made of a combination of sea mist with the smoke of innumerable coal fires; they penetrated the inside of London houses even when the windows were tightly shut, and when the fog lifted everything was grimy and there was an acrid smell. In Wallis's house there was no central heating, but it had a coal fire in every room. This extremely gloomy winter lowered her usually high spirits and began to get her down. Simpson was meticulous and once a week they went through the household books together. Perhaps Wallis thought this too was an old English custom, like reading the Court Circular in *The Times* to see what the King and Queen had been up to. How was she to know that Simpson was unique, with his ledger and his tiny writing making a note of every ounce of sugar or pound of hake? 'There was no trace of the skylark in Ernest Simpson,' wrote Wallis.

When spring came, the Simpsons were planning to go abroad for a holiday, but Wallis got a cable from Aunt Bessie to say her mother was seriously ill. They went to Washington; this was the first time Ernest had met his mother-in-law. They liked each other, and she was obviously relieved to see that Wallis had settled down with such a solid, sensible person. After three sad weeks Aunt Bessie made Wallis go back to England; the doctor said her mother might live for several years more. Simpson, who had left long before, met her at Southampton. England in June was lovely, and he planned a series of journeys to show her the cathedrals and castles he so much admired. Every week-end they motored to a new sight-seeing centre. That summer they also looked round for a London house of their own, and finally took a flat in a new block, Bryanston Court. For the first time in her life Wallis had her own home and was able to furnish and arrange it in her own way. She bought old furniture and made the rather unpromising flat cheerful and pretty. She was beginning to make friends, but so far she had not really had a good time in London; English people are harder to get to know than Americans or than the foreign colony in Peking and Shanghai.

A call from Aunt Bessie in October made her dash over to America once again, but she only arrived in time to see her mother die, on 2 November 1929. She was very sad; her mother was one of the few people Wallis really loved. Aunt Bessie was another.

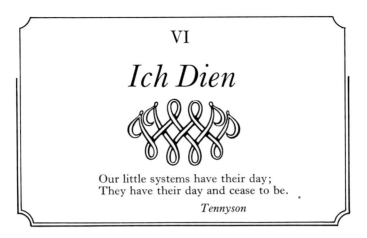

# VI

## *Ich Dien*

Our little systems have their day;
They have their day and cease to be.

*Tennyson*

After the war, even in England, things had changed. Lord Cromer wrote: 'In spite of the increasing labours and devotion to public duty of the King and Queen during the last three years the fact remains that the position of the Monarchy is not so stable now, in 1918, as it was at the beginning of the War. ... No stone should be left unturned in the endeavour to consolidate the position of the Crown. The Crown is the link of Empire and its fate is inseparable from that of all British Possessions.' So it seemed at the time; nobody then foresaw that less than half a century later Britain would have virtually no 'Possessions', but that the island would cling tenaciously to its traditions and its Monarchy.

The stone King George decided to turn, with the encouragement of Lloyd George, was the popularity of his heir. Lord Esher had written in his diary in 1915 of a talk he had with Queen Mary. 'She is proud of the Prince of Wales. I tried to make her see that after the War thrones might be at a discount, and that the Prince of Wales's popularity might be a great asset.' After 1918 it was obvious that Lord Esher was right, and the King resolved that the 'great asset' should be used to cement the Empire and strengthen its ties with the mother country. He sent the Prince away on a series of tours of the Empire, each of which in those days of travel by sea took months of his life.

Wherever he went he was greeted by vast, cheering crowds; there were endless banquets and balls and ceremonies of every kind at which all eyes were upon him. Every word he spoke was treasured, repeated, commented upon. People who saw him, or met him, or talked with him, were 'charmed into raptures', just as the grumpy French general on the Italian front had been. He looked so young with his gold hair and china blue eyes and his

*The Prince of Wales with Winston Churchill outside the House of Commons in 1919.
Between the two men there was a strong bond of affection*

*Left: The Prince of Wales meeting the officers at Annapolis Naval Academy during his visit to America in 1919. His right hand had become so swollen that he was obliged to shake hands with his left hand*

*Below: The Prince during his visit to America. This photograph was to become his wife's favourite*

smile – young and also vulnerable. In fact he was quite tough and he had the family obstinacy, but his boyish and vulnerable appearance was another asset, arousing as it did chivalrous as well as maternal feelings in the thousands of men and women in the crowds.

When he was in a carriage or motor car driving through the throng people did not confine themselves to cheering. Particularly in Australia, the unfortunate Prince would hear the shrill cry: 'I touched him!' over and over again. 'Owing to the hearty disposition of the Australians the touches are more like blows, and HRH and Admiral Halsey arrived half blinded and black and blue,' wrote a member of his staff. The Prince's right hand became so swollen and sore that it had to be bandaged and he shook hands with his left. In Canada too his reception was violently enthusiastic. Huge crowds gathered, and 'again and again they broke through and swamped the police lines' wrote the Prince. 'They snatched my handkerchief, they tried to tear the buttons off my coat.'

From Canada he went to visit ex-servicemen in America, and in New York he was given a ticker-tape welcome. He said that it was thrilling beyond description. Through the snow-storm of ticker-tape and torn-up telephone books he rode on the back of a motor 'bowing and waving like an actor who has been summoned by a tremendous curtain call'. He possessed in supreme degree the royal grace of memorizing faces and putting names to them, so that nobody was ever hurt at being forgotten, since he forgot nobody.

After the war all the royal family's German relations had lost their thrones and rights and positions; the little German courts made fun of by Thackeray long ago were but shadows, the Reich a republic. A Protestant wife had to be found for the Prince, but marriage with a German princess would have been highly unpopular as a result of the war and its attendant unbridled anti-German propaganda. For the King and Queen this question of the Prince's marriage was a constant, nagging worry. While he was away on his tours the worry receded, only to become acute once more on his return. Some of the older friends of the royal family ventured to speak to him on the subject, and he said to Lady Salisbury, his equerry Bruce Ogilvy's aunt: 'It's no good, Lady Salisbury. Bruce and I are two old bachelors. Neither of us will ever marry any woman unless we really love her.'

The most interesting of his tours was his visit to India. Before he left, the King told him that the sort of democratic behaviour he had indulged in hitherto would be quite out of place in India; it would be misunderstood. He enjoined the Prince, as he so often had before, but with renewed emphasis, 'Never forget who you are'. He sailed for the Far East in the *Renown*, a squash court had been built in the ship so that he could get some exercise on the voyage. Captain Ogilvy went with him. 'We saw and did everything. We stayed with all the Governors and a great many of the Maharajas . . . the latter like an Arabian Night's dream. The most fantastic luxury and the jewels out of this world.' They hunted every sort of animal, including rhino. It was in India that the Prince made the acquaintance of Major 'Fruity' Metcalfe, who became a great friend and equerry.

The exhausting Empire tours were considered a tremendous success, but they left him with not only the desire but the absolute need for a time of relative solitude during which he could renew his strength before setting forth once again. It was during these rests, when he hunted in Leicestershire or danced at the Embassy Club, that King George pestered him with advice and admonitions. Everything was wrong, particularly the Prince's clothes if in some tiny way they differed from the King's own conservative style of dressing. His friends were not the very ones his father would have chosen for him. Because the King himself always went to bed at eleven he considered this was the proper time and that to stay up later was almost immoral. The very word 'night-club' was abhorrent to the King. Edward VII had been fond of the Marlborough Club, but that was a day club and for men only. George V felt no need for a club of any kind whether by day or by night, and to him a night-club sounded almost orgiastic and not at all the sort of place where the heir to the throne should spend his evenings.

The Embassy Club in Bond Street was perfectly respectable, but the King had naturally never seen it and to him it was dissolute. As if by magic he always seemed to know when the Prince, often accompanied by his favourite brother Prince George, had been there. The all-seeing eye was apparently provided by Evelyn Duchess of Devonshire,* Queen Mary's Mistress of the Robes, whose informant was perhaps her youngest son, Lord Charles Cavendish. If in all innocence he told his mother where the Princes had been seen the night before, she quickly told the Queen, who told the King, who could not resist scolding, although his son was now thirty.

The King doubtless thought there were still, despite the war, enough great houses in London where the Princes were invited to balls and parties, and where their fellow-guests came from England's old families. Why did they have to go to the Embassy Club? He failed to understand why a party of six friends should be a

*This suspicion was told to the author years later by the Duke of Windsor. The present Duchess of Devonshire, who was also there, asked him 'Was she nasty when you met her face to face?' and the Duke laughed. '*Nasty*? Smarmy as be damned', he said.

relaxation for the Prince in a way that a ball where he was a centre of attention could never be. The Prince obstinately insisted that his private life was his own, a source of annoyance to his parents all through the twenties.

After Princess Mary's marriage to Lord Lascelles in 1922 the Prince of Wales's brother Bertie, now Duke of York, wrote to him: 'Papa and Mama will miss her too terribly, I fear, but it may have a good effect in bringing them out again. I feel they can't possibly stay in and dine together every night of their lives.' But this is what the King and Queen did, it was what the King liked to do.

The Prince of Wales, because of what they called 'David's fads', among which was his 'tiresome golf', came in for a good deal of criticism. He no longer lived in 'the awful palace' but had arranged York House, embedded in St James's, for himself. He described it as 'a rambling, antiquated structure, a veritable rabbit warren with passages interrupted by unexpected flights of steps leading to unsymmetrical rooms full of ugly Victorian furniture, brass beds and discarded portraits of former Monarchs '.

He appointed two equerries,* Lord Claud Hamilton and Captain Piers Legh, son of Lord Newton. Another equerry, Bruce Ogilvy, has described the Prince's life at York House.

My first job in the morning was to play squash with HRH at the Bath Club with a heat bath and massage after. He was mad keen on keeping fit and wore about five sweaters and the result was that any indiscretions of the night before were well eliminated! After that, various interviews with all sorts of different people. The equerry on duty had to keep them talking until he was ready to see them, and that could be interesting. After interviews, lunch out as no meals except breakfast were provided at York House. Then probably nothing till the evening, when one accompanied him to some public dinner where he had to speak. He spoke very well and though the speeches were provided by Godfrey [Thomas] and Tommy [Lascelles]** he often put in remarks, generally very shrewd, of his own. After official duties for the evening were finished one was free to pursue one's own night life. He always had a special table reserved for him at the Embassy Club.

There was plenty of hard work for the Prince when he was in England, and in the time he had to himself he continued to see his friends and people he liked who were not always considered 'suitable' by the palace, people who amused him or who had simply

*During a visit to America the Prince was asked by Will Rogers what an 'equerry' was; he tried to explain, and Will Rogers said: 'Well, Sir, I guess we have the same animal out in Oklahoma, only we call 'em hired hands.'
**Private secretaries.

become familiar enough so that he felt at ease with them. To the Prince, the most important of these friends was Mrs Dudley Ward, a delightful young woman who had two little daughters. He loved the whole family and saw for the first time at close quarters what devotion between a mother and her children could be. His happiest hours were spent with Mrs Dudley Ward, he often dropped in for a chat or they dined with a few friends. Once when he invited her to his box at the Albert Hall for the annual Remembrance Day ceremony, during community singing of

Hullo! Hullo! Who's your lady friend?
Who's the little lady by your side?

the great audience of ex-servicemen stood up laughing and clapping and cheering and faced the Prince of Wales's box where he sat with Mrs Dudley Ward.

In his history of English fox-hunting Raymond Carr says the Prince was 'a bold horseman'. He has himself described the fun he had hunting with the Beaufort and then with the great Leicestershire packs. He stayed at Craven Lodge, Melton Mowbray, a club founded by Captain Mike Wardell, where his horses were stabled. A neighbour at Melton, Monica Sherriffe, remembers the Prince: 'He was always very friendly and fun out hunting. Madly brave and loved by all the farmers. He was so marvellous looking with that golden hair, and fascinating cockney voice.'* Bruce Ogilvy, who often hunted with him, says he was 'courageous, loved jumping fences but knew absolutely nothing about hound work. Unless he had had a fall he was always there or thereabouts at the end of a hunt.' Unfortunately for him, every time he had a fall it made front-page news, with the result that there was a general impression that he never stopped falling. It became a music hall joke. Even in America, Cole Porter wrote a song called 'Let's Fall in Love', which contained the lines:

Snails do it, quails do it,
Horses that have thrown the Prince of Wales do it,
Let's do it, let's fall in love.

When he took to riding in point-to-points journalists and photographers gathered in the hope he would fall. He won a race at Hawthorn Hill, but in the Army point-to-point their wish was granted; he fell on his head and was concussed. This was the signal for a letter from the King, in March 1924, telling him to give up steeple-chasing. He must have had the impression that whenever he enjoyed doing something it was banned by the King.

That summer he went to Long Island with a polo team. In the evenings there were parties, and his every move was accompanied

*Letter to the author.

*Mrs Dudley Ward*

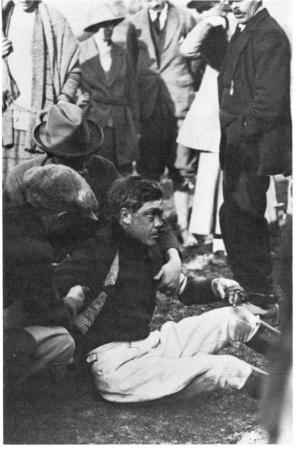

*The Prince of Wales riding in a point-to-point in March 1924. The race ended with a bad fall (left) provoking a letter from the King telling him to give up steeple-chasing*

by typical American publicity, something which in those days was only just beginning in England. Headlines like 'PRINCE GETS IN WITH MILKMAN', or 'HERE HE IS GIRLS – THE MOST ELIGIBLE BACHELOR YET UNCAUGHT', were typical. When he got back to London and went to see his father, he found him with a heap of American newspaper cuttings. King George was outraged by their effrontery. The Prince tried vainly to calm him, saying Americans pay little attention to newspaper headlines. Henceforward the King, while avoiding an outright ukase, saw to it that his sons did not go to America; he put irremovable obstacles in their way. This the Prince regretted; he loved America and considered it the country of the future. One piece of effrontery had not hit the headlines. When a newspaper reporter asked the Prince whether if he fell in love with an American girl he would marry her, the laughter which greeted the question drowned the answer. It was 'yes'.

Not only in America did the Prince get in with the milk. Bruce Ogilvy, his equerry at Windsor Castle during Ascot week, wrote:

> He hated it. The guests for the week were not at all young and on the whole not very gay. I used to enjoy it. The food and rum rations were of course super and one could always have a ride or a game of tennis or squash in the morning before going racing.
>
> The evenings were very dull. Penny poker usually, after dinner. Once or twice during the week after everybody had gone to bed HRH and I motored up to London and met Freda Dudley Ward and some of her friends at her house and we used to dance to the gramophone and have supper. On one occasion we were motoring back in the small hours, the Prince driving his own car. There was practically no traffic and he was driving at the rate of knots when a large lorry came out of a side road and very nearly collided with us. The Prince by a brilliant bit of driving switched onto the grass verge. We skidded and bumped along for about three hundred yards, eventually getting back on the tarmac safely. I have often wondered what the headlines in the paper next day would have been had there been a bad accident.

It was Captain Ogilvy's duty 'to warn the Guard not to turn out in the small hours when HRH returned'.

Bruce Ogilvy's mother, Mabell Lady Airlie, was always in waiting at Windsor for Ascot: 'I used to go and see her every morning after breakfast and I told her all the goings-on of the night before.' But unlike the Duchess of Devonshire, Lady Airlie told no tales.

# VII

# Mrs Simpson meets the Prince

'Come, come', said Tom's father, 'at your time
of life
There's no longer excuse for thus playing the
rake;
It is time you should think, boy, of taking a
wife,'
'Why, so it is, father – whose wife shall I take?'

*Tom Moore*

After two years living in London, Wallis, now aged thirty-four, had made some English friends, and she also saw many visiting Americans as well as American diplomats *en poste* in London. Among the latter was Benjamin Thaw, First Secretary of the US Embassy, who was married to Consuelo Morgan. Mrs Thaw's sisters were Gloria Vanderbilt and Thelma Lady Furness, the Prince of Wales's friend of the moment. Wallis's favourite cousin Corinne was also in London with her new husband, Lieutenant Commander Murray, Assistant Naval Attaché. Wallis had an excellent cook and she gave small dinner parties at Bryanston Court; also she was at home every evening at six when she made American cocktails for anyone who cared to drop in. As the old American song says: 'Good times were round the corner.'

Mrs Simpson met the Prince of Wales through the Benjamin Thaws. They were to have been guests of Mrs Thaw's sister, Lady Furness, in the country the following week-end when the Prince was expected, but Mrs Thaw had to leave for Paris because her mother-in-law had been taken ill there. They begged Wallis to take her place as chaperon. Although she was dying to meet the Prince, of whom she had heard constantly during her two years in London, Wallis at first refused. She would not know what to say to him, or how to curtsy, and it was a hunting week-end and she knew nothing about hunting. Mrs Thaw insisted; Benny Thaw would take the Simpsons down to Leicestershire and look after them in every way, she said. When Wallis told Mr Simpson about the invitation he was overjoyed; he said it was a great honour and they must certainly accept. Lady Furness telephoned to thank them for solving her problem, and on Friday afternoon they met Mr Thaw at St Pancras and took the train to Melton. On the journey Wallis made Mr Thaw show her how to curtsy; together they wobbled on the floor of the railway carriage.

A drive through dripping fog took them to the Furness hunting box, a modern, comfortable house. Wallis, who had a cold and felt a slight temperature coming on, wished she could go to bed, but when the Prince of Wales appeared the cold was quickly forgotten. Wearing loud checked tweeds he was accompanied by Brigadier General 'G' Trotter and by Prince George, who soon left because he was staying in the neighbourhood with other friends.

Wallis says she was surprised to discover that the Prince was so small. The royal family had inherited tiny stature from Queen Victoria; in those days 'king size' meant something miniature. She noticed his blue eyes, in which she detected a rather sad expression. She admired his natural, easy manners and the way he put everyone else at ease; she decided that he was one of the most attractive people she had ever met in her life. 'Do you suppose he'll ever marry?' she asked Benny Thaw, who replied that he had been in love with several women and added: 'I rather doubt that he'll ever marry now, having waited so long.' As the Prince was only thirty-six Mr Thaw's guess, which as we know was wide of the mark, may seem rather strange.

This visit to Lady Furness was in the autumn of 1930. That winter the Prince of Wales in his role of 'Empire salesman' left England for a lengthy tour of South America; he had learned Spanish for the occasion. Wallis saw the Prince twice more during 1931, both times at the Grosvenor Square house of Lady Furness. Once he gave her and Mr Simpson a lift home in his car and she invited him and General Trotter to come in for a drink, but they were on their way to Fort Belvedere. Wallis had been presented at Court, quite a feat for a divorced woman. She borrowed the dress and feathers from Mrs Thaw and Lady Furness and was photographed looking very elegant. It was the following January, 1932, that a note came from the Prince inviting the Simpsons to stay at the Fort.

At this juncture it may be well to pause and look back at the story so far. As the whole world knows, the visit of Mrs Simpson and her husband to Fort Belvedere was to set in train a series of events which had grave consequences and caused a constitutional crisis of the first magnitude. Why this should have been is hard to understand; the reason lay deep in the character of the Prince himself and he is far and away the most important actor in the coming drama.

We have seen that his parents married because they were persuaded that it was their duty to do so. They became fond of one another but their feelings towards their children were mixed. The

69

Queen, while admitting that the Prince made a quite exceptional impact on people wherever he went, and even admiring him for it, could not understand him. They were not in sympathy, she would have preferred a prince more aloof from his future subjects, less democratic. In the matter of friends, from her point of view he had gone from bad to worse. It must have seemed to her that he deliberately turned his back on suitable friends and on the English aristocracy. With her romantic view of royalty as a race apart she would have wished him to marry a royal princess, but since the war had made such a match difficult she would have been quite happy for it to be with a lady of noble birth. She had suffered in her youth from the fact of her father's morganatic birth, and that she herself was not considered *ebenbürtig* by German princelings, but she had drawn first prize in the royal raffle by marrying the future King of England and she was conscious of playing her part perfectly. How doubly annoying, therefore, were 'David's fads', one of which was his unaccountable liking for Americans. Instead of seriously looking about him for a wife he spent his spare time with Lady Furness, the American wife of a rich ship owner. The Queen was well aware that rich people of lowly birth had appealed to her father-in-law King Edward VII, but he was married to a royal princess and the succession was assured by the time he went yachting with his grocer, as his nephew the Emperor William II had disobligingly described his outings with Sir Thomas Lipton. She and King George V saw very few people except in the way of duty, but their household was composed of ladies and gentlemen of impeccable antecedents. She doubtless felt annoyed with the Prince in a number of small ways, particularly for dressing in what the King considered an *outré* fashion, with loud checks, turn-up trousers and enormous plus-fours. Her second son, the Duke of York, never teased his father in this way; furthermore the Duke had married Lady Elizabeth Bowes-Lyon, and they had two little daughters, the older of whom was the apple of her grandfather's eye. Queen Mary was anxious about the Prince of Wales, so charming and yet so obstinate. With her almost religious reverence for the Throne she could never understand why, even if her son might not feel obliged to do as his *father* wished about the width of his trousers, he did not immediately obey his *King*.

The King's feelings about his heir were different, and verged on dislike. He disliked his way of talking, his cockney accent,* his way of dressing (clothes as the outward and visible sign of what was conventional and traditional were of the utmost importance to the King), his choice of friends, his pastimes, and above all his

*It was a faint, but unmistakable cockney accent. For example, he pronounced 'lady' almost 'lidy'. In later life he acquired certain American intonations.

*Above: Wallis in her flat at Bryanston Court in London*

*Right: Wearing dress and feathers borrowed from Consuelo Thaw and Thelma, Lady Furness, Wallis was presented at Court*

*Above: The Prince in outlandish golfing attire – blue check shirt, grey plus-fours and check stockings – so disliked by his father, the King. In this match he played against Lady Astor in the semi-final of the Parliamentary handicap at Walton Heath, 1933*

*Left: The Prince playing the bagpipes*

undoubted popularity. If the older generation of the aristocracy, taking a cue from the King, sometimes secretly criticized the Prince of Wales, ordinary people, and particularly ex-servicemen, adored him. With a look or a word he managed to convey infinite sympathy and understanding in a way that was quite new in a royal personage. He combined the royal magic with the common touch, and no other member of the royal family came anywhere near him for magic.

The other principal personage in the coming drama was Wallis herself. She had hardly changed during the last years and was as thin as ever, which suited the fashions of the day. Her dark hair was plainly dressed, with a centre parting. Her clothes were simple but smart, already she bought them in Paris.

Since her careful and lady-like upbringing Wallis had not had an easy life, but her second marriage, though unromantic, had solved pressing problems. She was no longer homeless or penniless. She had an affectionate husband who appreciated her many qualities. He admired her talent for making friends, and the fact that her dinner parties were so successful and enjoyable and the food she provided so much praised. She collected interesting people, and with her gaiety and high spirits she made everything go with a swing. Now here she was arranging for them to stay with the Prince of Wales, an undreamed-of honour in Ernest Simpson's eyes. They realized that the idea of the invitation had probably come from Lady Furness, but that did not detract from the glamour. Wallis was not nearly as excited about it as Mr Simpson, who, like Queen Mary, looked upon royalty as a race apart, and who could hardly believe his luck.

# VIII

# *The Prince in Love*

Krone des Lebens,
Glück ohne Ruh'
Liebe, bist du!
*Goethe*

Fort Belvedere is a grace and favour house belonging to the Crown situated six miles from Windsor Castle. It is a castellated eighteenth-century folly, added to by Wyatville. The Prince had asked his father if he might have it. 'What could you possibly want that old place for?' said the King. 'Those damn week-ends I suppose.' However he let the Prince have it, and the Fort became his home, where he did as he liked when he was off duty, and had his friends to stay. He made it comfortable inside and put Canalettos in the drawing room and horse pictures by Stubbs in the dining room, but his joy was the garden, over-grown and neglected, which he was gradually transforming into his very own paradise.

This first week-end with the Simpsons was a great success, though the unfortunate Ernest, who detested physical exertion, was roped in to help the Prince cut down and clear away untidy old laurels which disfigured the garden. When he hesitated, General 'G' Trotter told him: 'It's not a command but I've never known anyone refuse.' Simpson joined the laurel-slashers. In the evenings the Prince did his embroidery, he told Wallis he had learnt how to do *gros point* from Queen Mary. Then they danced to the gramophone. Wallis was impressed by the Prince's simple tastes and by the relaxed atmosphere at the Fort. She found the Prince of Wales extraordinarily attractive, but there was no question of a *coup de foudre* on either side. It was a friendship which gradually developed. She and her husband were invited to the Fort several times in 1933, and when it was realized that they had become friends with the Prince they began to be asked to dinners and parties by dozens of English people who would never have noticed them in the ordinary way. When Wallis spent two months in America the news had reached Maryland, and already there was an atmosphere of local-girl-makes-good in Baltimore.

*Fort Belvedere, an eighteenth-century folly in Windsor Great Park, described by the Prince as a 'pseudo-Gothic hodge-podge' The gardens at Fort Belvedere were wild and overgrown (right). One of the Prince's favourite occupations was to clear the laurels – an enthusiasm not shared by his guest, Ernest Simpson*

*Above: A tea party at the Fort, 1934. From left to right, Euan Wallace, Wallis, Evelyn Fitzgerald, Barbie Wallace, the Prince, Hugh Lloyd Thomas, and Mrs Fitzgerald*

*Left: Thelma, Lady Furness*

Back in London early in 1934 Lady Furness told her that she was going to America with her twin sister Gloria Vanderbilt for six weeks. 'Oh Thelma, the little man is going to be so lonely,' said Wallis. 'You look after him for me,' was the reply. While Lady Furness crossed the Atlantic in a glare of publicity with Aly Khan showering red roses and other attentions upon her, Wallis looked after the Prince. She gave little dinner parties for him at Bryanston Court, and she encouraged him to talk about his work. 'Wallis,' he told her, 'You are the only woman who has ever been interested in my job.' The Bryanston Court flat became his home from home. Whenever he had time he dropped in for a chat and a drink and stayed on and on, often until Mr Simpson got back from his office and they had to suggest dinner. Rather quickly Wallis became indispensable to him and he lived for the moments when they could be together.

By the time Lady Furness returned from America Wallis was firmly established as the Prince's greatest friend. She was not only a sympathetic and affectionate companion when they were alone, she could also be the liveliest and most amusing person at a party, the one who made everything more fun. Moreover she had what was for the Prince a unique attribute, her complete naturalness. It was something she never lost. She was probably the only woman he had ever met who did not feel obliged to behave slightly differently because he was there to the way she would have with anyone else. The Prince was one of the most sensitive beings ever born and he detected the falseness in people's approach to him immediately. He liked Americans because they were less awed by his position than English people were apt to be, but even with them there was as a rule the desire to impress, or to be impressed, or even to make naturalness into an act which he could see through.

Wallis was quite different. She was always very polite, curtsying, calling him 'Sir', but she always spoke her mind. It must have made him feel that at long last here was someone who treated him as he would have wished. To the end of his life he remained 'very royal' (in the words of Lord Tennyson, whose parents had been friends of the Prince and who saw him often in France during the fifties and sixties). He never allowed people to be casual or off-hand with him, let alone impertinent or insolent. He wanted exactly what Wallis gave him, natural and unaffected good manners.

At the same time he was very much attracted by her. She was his type of woman, small and thin, beautifully dressed. He admired her efficiency, the trouble she took about details. And he loved her jokes and her wise cracks and her rapid response to the jokes of others, her irrepressible gaiety. She could talk, and she could listen. Like him, she learnt from people what can hardly be learnt from books. He fell deeply, obsessively and permanently in love with her; it happened gradually and once it had happened he remained in love with her until the day he died. He was constant as the northern star.

Bruce Ogilvy writes: 'After Thelma Furness had realized that all was over between her and the Prince of Wales, 'G' Trotter, who was a friend of hers, took her out to dinner and of course talked about the whole affair. The Prince got to hear of this and had 'G' Trotter up and just sacked him on the spot because of what he had said to Thelma Furness. I think it really broke G's heart because he had been very fond of the Prince of Wales and really a great friend.' This was the first of a series of rather heartless actions on the part of the Prince, who could not tolerate even the faintest disloyalty, or what he chose to look upon as disloyalty, towards Wallis. His love for her filled him to the exclusion of all else, even of old friendships.

Although the great public knew nothing of the Prince of Wales's friendship with Mrs Simpson a fairly wide circle in London knew of it, and those who did thought at first it was just Lady Furness over again and Wallis the Prince's latest American friend. Society being what it is, Wallis began to have not just a good time but the time of her life. She was courted and flattered. Mr Simpson, however, knew very well that if the Simpsons had become such a centre of attraction for all the snobs in London it was certainly not because of him. He absented himself more and more, and in fact behaved with dignity.

Rumours of the romance reached Buckingham Palace, but probably beyond regretting one more obstacle to a suitable marriage the Queen at first paid no attention. As we shall see, the King's attitude was completely different from hers.

In the summer of 1934 the Prince took a villa at Biarritz and invited Wallis, with her Aunt Bessie as chaperon. They had not been there very long when Lord Moyne appeared in his yacht. His companion was Posy, wife of his cousin Kenelm Guinness. Lord Moyne invited the Prince and Wallis to cruise with them to the Mediterranean. He was an intrepid sailor and took them through some very rough weather, but they eventually reached calm seas and anchored off Formentor, a beautiful beach on the enchanted island of Majorca, in those days a lonely paradise.

Wallis wrote in her memoirs that the cruise on *Rosaura* was a turning point. The Prince was now undoubtedly in love with her. 'Searching my mind I could find no good reason why this most glamorous of men should be seriously attracted to me,' she says modestly. 'I certainly was no beauty, and he had the pick of the beautiful women of the world. I was certainly no longer very young. In fact in my own country I would have been considered securely on the shelf [Wallis was now thirty-eight]'. She goes on to give the reason for this interest in her: directness, independence of spirit, sense of humour. 'Perhaps it was this naturalness of attitude that had first astonished, then amazed and finally amused him.' Amused? Maybe, but captivated certainly. 'Then too he was lonely and perhaps I had been one of the first to penetrate the heart of his inner loneliness, his sense of separateness.' All true, no doubt, and Wallis had other qualities which she does not mention, one of which was courage. What she lacked was an understanding of England and English life and English ways, but however expertly she had surveyed the situation in which she found herself the end result would have been the same.

When he got home, the Prince composed a tune (if that is the right word) for the bagpipes, dedicated to Wallis. During his short stay at Balmoral he practised it near the castle until the King threw open a window and shouted at him to stop. There was evidently something about this particular melody that he disliked; none of the royal family minded the sound of bagpipes, and the Prince was addicted to them and played after dinner at the Fort.

Aunt Bessie asked her niece straight out whether the Prince was 'rather taken' with her. 'These old eyes aren't so old that they can't see what's in every glance.' Wallis tried to reassure her aunt, 'I know what I'm doing,' but Mrs Merryman said: 'Wiser people than you have been carried away, and I can see no happy outcome to such a situation.'

That autumn the Prince's favourite brother and companion, Prince George, now Duke of Kent, married Princess Marina of Greece; the Prince of Wales became lonelier than ever and more dependent upon Wallis. The Simpsons were invited to all the wedding festivities and at the reception at Buckingham Palace the Prince brought Mrs Simpson up to the Queen, saying: 'I want to introduce a great friend of mine.' The Queen shook hands without thinking much about it, but two years later she said to Lady Airlie: 'If I had only guessed then I might perhaps have been able to do something, but now it's too late.'

In February 1935, Mrs Simpson and the Prince of Wales went to ski at Kitzbühl, taking Bruce Ogilvy and his wife Primrose and sister-in-law Olive. It was not a great success. Wallis made no attempt to learn to ski, so from Kitzbühl they went on to Vienna and Budapest. There was nothing the Prince enjoyed more than

*The Prince with Wallis at Biarritz in August 1934: their first holiday together*

*The skiing party at Kitzbühl, February 1935. The Prince and Wallis are on the left, on the right is the Prince's former equerry, Bruce Ogilvy. The two ladies standing in the centre are Primrose Ogilvy and her sister Olive*

singing German songs and waltzing to the music of Lehar and Strauss.

This was the year of King George V's Silver Jubilee; there were great demonstrations of love and loyalty all over England. The King was reported to have said: 'They really seem to like me for myself.' The truth is that the British people in the great majority love their Kings and Queens, they love hanging out flags and seeing processions and other excitements. Nineteen-thirty-five was a year when there was still terrible unemployment and widespread misery, and the free spectacle cheered everyone up while it lasted.

Edward VII, so unlike his son, would have had exactly the same enthusiastic reception had he lived long enough to celebrate a jubilee. Queen Victoria, who was in every imaginable way the opposite of Edward VII, was acclaimed at her Golden Jubilee and then at her Diamond Jubilee, and she was confidently expected to live for ever (see the Coronation service: 'May the Queen live for ever') so that her death caused consternation as well as sorrow. In England there is no such thing as a typical monarch, the fact that for long past each has been unlike the predecessor has not mattered in the least, one and all seem perfect to most of their subjects. The old joke

> There's a divinity doth hedge a king
> Rough-hew him how we will,*

contains an important truth.

This loyal love is not extended to other members of the royal family, who are freely criticized, often with notable unfairness, though even now the gutter press is not so nasty as it was in Queen Victoria's reign, when the birth of a prince or a princess to the Queen was greeted with complaints about yet another pensioner to be paid for from the public funds.

The Prince of Wales took Lord Cholmondeley's villa at Cannes for his summer holiday that year. Besides Wallis he invited Lord and Lady Brownlow, Lord Sefton and a few other friends; his equerry was Major Jack Aird. They did not stay all the time at the villa, the Duke of Westminster took them for a cruise in his yacht, and they borrowed *Sister Anne*, Mrs Reginald Fellowes' boat, for a trip to Porquerolles. Then they went back to Vienna, a journey which had to be arranged on the spur of the moment by Major Aird, with *wagons-lits* for the whole party. Wallis marvelled at the way difficulties vanished when the Prince wanted something; it evidently gave her a feeling of his omnipotence. She was also becoming accustomed to being warmly welcomed wherever she went, and with her frank and open nature she probably began to

*1066 and All That.

81

*King George V's Silver Jubilee was celebrated in May 1935. Left: the King and Queen drive up Ludgate Hill to take part in the thanksgiving service in St Paul's Cathedral. Above: more modest celebrations in a Stepney backstreet. The King was heard to say: 'They really seem to like me for myself'*

imagine, like George V, that people liked her for herself. After all, she had always been popular and nothing in her life hitherto had prepared her for what was in store.

The King disapproved of Mediterranean holidays and thought the Prince should content himself with Balmoral, where the royal family gathered in August. Bruce Ogilvy writes: 'I used to accompany the Prince to Balmoral, where he stayed as short a time as possible. We used to go out stalking which he liked better than grouse driving as he got more exercise at it. It was sad that he and his father did not get on better, but it was the same with all his brothers and sister. King George V was a good king but a very unsympathetic father.'

Lady Airlie says that in her opinion 'the Prince's behaviour when his father hauled him over the coals for being the "worst-dressed man in London" and laid traps for him with orders and decorations, showed the utmost forbearance'. It is not surprising that the Prince chose to put a thousand miles between himself and his father at holiday time, particularly since one of the guests at Balmoral was Cosmo Lang, the Archbishop of Canterbury, who loved gossiping with the King about his heir. The Archbishop drove over to Airlie for luncheon and told Lady Airlie how concerned the King and Queen were about the Prince's 'latest friendship'. 'His Majesty believes that this affair is much more serious than the others. That is what worries him.'

The following winter the King, who had been ailing for some time, became seriously ill. The whole family including the Prince of Wales gathered at Sandringham for Christmas; early in January 1936 the King died, just forty-four years after Prince Eddy had died in the same house. A few weeks before his death the King had exclaimed passionately to the Queen, in front of Lady Algernon Gordon-Lennox,* a very old friend: 'I pray to God that my eldest son will never marry and have children and that nothing will come between Bertie and Lilibet and the throne.'

The Prince had certainly not earned this fierce resentment on the part of his father. Compared with Edward VII when he was Prince of Wales his conduct had been exemplary. He had worked very hard both at home and in his Empire tours. He had never, as his grandfather had more than once, figured in a public scandal or been obliged to give evidence in a squalid court case. It is difficult to resist the thought that in part the King's dislike was due to jealousy. He felt no jealousy of the Duke of York, and he loved his nine-year-old granddaughter. As we know, a large part of his prayer was destined to be answered.

*She repeated it to Mabell Lady Airlie, who immediately noted it down.

84

## IX

# *Loved by a King*

I awoke one morning and found myself famous

*Byron*

The new King invited Wallis and a few other friends to watch the picturesque ceremony of the Proclamation of the Accession of King Edward VIII from a window in St James's Palace. To her astonishment he himself suddenly appeared at her side. When the solemn and moving ceremony was over, and the Guards band had played 'God Save the King', they went downstairs together. 'This has made me realize how different your life is going to be,' said Wallis, to which he replied: 'Wallis, there will be a difference of course. But nothing can ever change my feelings towards you.' Then with a sudden smile he was gone.

The new King was busy from morning till night. As Prince of Wales he had always worked hard; it was after work that he had acquired the habit of calling at Bryanston Court to see Wallis rather than sitting at York House with the equerries. There were now endless things to be seen to and duties to perform. The Court was in mourning, but when spring came the 'damn week-ends' at the Fort continued as before, whenever the King could get away. The same group of people was invited: the Brownlows, Buists, Lord Sefton and the future Lady Sefton (who was an old American friend of Wallis's, 'Foxie' Gwynne), also the Duff Coopers, Anthony Edens and Euan Wallaces. Euan Wallace was a well-known Conservative Member of Parliament, Barbie Wallace (now Mrs Herbert Agar) a daughter of Sir Edwin Lutyens, describes a visit to the Fort that summer where they stayed several times. On arrival, guests were handed a card: 'Mourning will not be worn after 6 p.m.'

It was an Alice-in-Wonderland atmosphere and the only royal occasions I have ever enjoyed. I have always felt it's torture to be with royalty as one can't do right ... If one talks to them one's a snob, if one doesn't one's not pulling one's weight. With life at the Fort it was quite different. Wallis was very formal with the King, plenty of curtsies and Your Majesty, but managed to make everyone happy and at ease and of course delicious food. Wallis was a wonderful hostess and had the best manners I've ever seen. She always talked to everyone and even engaged Sir Arthur Colefax in animated conversation. No-one had ever spoken a word to him before.

This is a notable tribute, not only to Wallis's good manners but to her kindness. Sir Arthur Colefax was a famous bore; his wife was a lion-hunting hostess who caught plenty of lions, none of whom threw a word to their host. Lord Berners once said that the Government had offered Sir Arthur £30,000 'to bore the Channel Tunnel'.

Mrs Agar continues: 'After dinner everyone drove to Windsor Castle for a film, during which endless footmen in royal livery crawled about on all fours (in order not to spoil the view of the screen) offering champagne. When the lights went on most of the guests were asleep.'

Lady Diana Cooper has described the putting out and putting in of cushions and mattresses round the swimming pool when the sun shone fitfully. The King wanted everything at the Fort to be informal, but it never quite was. When he mixed the cocktails and poured them out himself nobody forgot for an instant that he was the King. Wallis did not forget, but she accepted it more easily than anyone else. She was the pivot, the centre, the person towards whom what Lord Louis Mountbatten called his magnetic charm was principally directed. There is no doubt that everyone enjoyed visits to the Fort.

It was in May that the King gave a dinner party at York House to which he invited the Simpsons and Mr and Mrs Stanley Baldwin. With his 'most Prince-Charming smile' he said to Wallis: 'It's got to be done. Sooner or later my Prime Minister must meet my future wife.' She immediately replied that any idea of her being his future wife was impossible and out of the question; 'They'd never let you.' 'I'm well aware of all that,' said the King, 'but rest assured, I will manage it somehow.' This is the first time marriage is mentioned in Wallis's memoirs, and for several more months she continued to deny that there was any question of such a thing between her and the King, but they must obviously have discussed it many times already. It appears that in 1934 he had already made up his mind to marry her.

The guests at the dinner, besides the Baldwins, were the Mountbattens, the Duff Coopers, Lady Cunard, the Lindberghs

*Above: The Garter King of Arms with the Duke of Norfolk, the Earl Marshal, reading the Proclamation of the Accession of Edward VIII from the balcony of Friary Court in St James's Palace, January 1936. Wallis watched from a window with the new King at her side*

*Left: Debutantes being presented to the King at Buckingham Palace in 1936. In order to get the whole business quickly finished, it was decided that the presentation should take place at a garden party; the occasion was ruined by rain. The King looked, and was, bored*

*Above: Photograph portrait of Edward VIII, which was to become the image of the King on postage stamps and coins*

*Below: The King setting out from Buckingham Palace for Hyde Park to present new colours to the Grenadier, Coldstream and the Scots Guards. On the King's way back to the Palace a man pushed through the police line and threw a loaded revolver at the royal horse – the King remained completely unmoved*

and Admiral Sir Ernle Chatfield and Lady Chatfield. The list appeared next day in the Court Circular, but Ernest Simpson did not savour it as he would have once. It was the last time he was the King's guest. He had found a sympathetic companion in Wallis's old friend Mary Kirk, Mme Raffray, who was soon to be the third Mrs Simpson. Since her marriage had now broken down Wallis decided to divorce. She asked the King for the name of a solicitor and he suggested Mr Theodore Goddard. 'From then on I acted on Mr Goddard's advice,' says Wallis. Whether his advice was always the very wisest is open to question. Mr Simpson left Bryanston Court and went to live at the Guards Club. Before bowing out of Wallis's life he had an interview with the King, and, like a Victorian father with his daughter's suitor, asked him his intentions.

Shortly afterwards the King gave another dinner party, for Sir Samuel and Lady Maud Hoare, the Duke and Duchess of York, David Margesson the Chief Whip, the Willingdons, the Winston Churchills, Lady Diana Cooper, Lady Colefax and Wallis, but this time there was no Ernest Simpson, a fact registered by readers of the Court Circular which, formerly so dull, had now become a source of endless gossip and conjecture in London society. Sir Samuel Hoare was intrigued to meet the famous Mrs Simpson about whom everyone was talking. He noted that she was 'very attractive and intelligent, very American and with little or no knowledge of English life'.

Among those who were incensed by the appearance of Mrs Simpson's name in the Court Circular was Lady Astor, an American from Virginia who said that only members of old families from the American South should be allowed to become acquainted with the royal family. This nuance passed most English people by. In any case, as we have seen, she was barking up the wrong tree. Wallis's family was very old by American standards, and her father's and mother's families both came from Southern States.

Noteworthy about these dinner parties given by the King is not so much that Mrs Simpson was present (the King would never have had a party without her) as that many of the guests were prominent Tory politicians. Wallis, an avid reader of newspapers and magazines, was very well-informed, and on the whole she much preferred the company of politicians to any other. Lady Cunard and Lady Colefax were hostesses who invited interesting people to meet her and the King, and in common courtesy they had to be asked back. With the exception of his own relations, an Admiral and Charles Lindbergh, all the men at these dinners were members of the Houses of Parliament. This was something of a new departure; the boon companions of yester-year were less in evidence. If someone was an old friend and also a politician, like Winston Churchill, so much the better.

Now that her Prince was King Wallis was determined that he should devote himself to serious matters; she did not understand that in England a political King could be in deep trouble, or that the Monarch must, as far as humanly possible, be above politics, sitting firmly on the fence. Edward VIII had strong views on a number of subjects; too strong. Wallis with her sketchy knowledge of English affairs never realized that he might be more safely employed with his 'tiresome golf' or even (in private) with the good times she had so rigorously put behind her. She observed that everyone deferred to him, that his will was law; she failed to understand how limited was his power.

Sir Samuel Hoare had been involved in a major political row because of the Hoare-Laval Pact which decreed that Britain and France were to lift sanctions against Italy and allow it to keep some of its conquests in Abyssinia. He had had to resign, but was now back in office, and it was perhaps rather typical that Edward VIII should give a dinner party for him. The King was, and remained, an Empire man. He probably thought Abyssinia would be better administered by Italians than by Haile Selassie. He had given years of his life to the British Empire, and he thought it absurd hypocrisy to deny colonies to other European powers, simply because they were acquiring them a few years later than the British.

From this time on the American press began printing more and more stories about the romance. What had previously been given the odd mention now and again became a steady stream of comment about the King of England and the lady from Baltimore. The English newspapers did not refer to it, and American publications appeared on the news stands with bits cut out of them, because of the threat of libel and vast damages which always hangs over the English distributors just as it does over writers and publishers.

Wallis continued to give small dinners at her flat to which people flocked in order to see the King and gauge the temperature of the romance. She invited Harold Nicolson, who wrote in his diary that Lady Oxford, Lady Cunard and Lady Colefax were all present and each of these noted personalities furious at the other two having been asked. 'Something snobbish in me is rather saddened by all this. Mrs Simpson is a perfectly harmless type of American, but the whole setting is slightly second rate.' This sour comment is reminiscent of Groucho Marx: 'I wouldn't want to join a club which would have me for a member.'

For his summer holiday the King chartered a yacht, the *Nahlin*,

*Wallis with her Cairn terrier, Pookie*

*The cruise on the* Nahlin *in the summer of 1936. Above: Wallis with the King at Pompeii. Below: Katherine Rogers with Wallis and the King at Portofino*

*Above: Lunch aboard the*
Nahlin, *with, on the left,*
*Wallis and the King of*
*Greece, and on the right,*
*the King and Mrs*
*Fitzgerald. Right: Wallis*
*on the bridge of the* Nahlin

and cruised along the Dalmatian coast, through the Corinth Canal via Athens to Istanbul, escorted by two destroyers. Besides Wallis he invited the Duff Coopers, Herman and Katherine Rogers, Lord Sefton and a few more, also the private secretaries Godfrey Thomas and Alan ('Tommy') Lascelles, with Jack Aird as equerry. Wherever the yacht appeared, crowds of people sprang from nowhere to welcome the King, and Mrs Simpson too. Even peasants from the remote villages in Jugoslavia seemed to know that the King was in love. Whenever he and Wallis went ashore they were mobbed by adoring throngs shouting: 'Long live the King!' and 'Long live love!' Wallis was astonished to find that what she had fondly imagined was her private life seemed to be known to the whole world, except, that is, in England, because the English newspapers had still published nothing at all about it. Whether or not the King was astonished he behaved in a recklessly indiscreet manner, always at Wallis's side. He saw no reason to conceal his feelings any more than have kings all through history.

When they dined with the King of Greece the host sat between Wallis and Lady Diana Cooper, who says Wallis was splendid, 'the wisecracks following in quick succession, the King [of Greece] clearly very admiring and amused'. At that time everyone was admiring and amused; Wallis wisely lived for the moment and did not peer into the future.

When the yacht reached Athens and King Edward was invited to meet the English colony at the British Legation Wallis refused to go too, saying his subjects wanted to see *him*. This put him in a bad humour, but he probably realized she was right. He says in his memoirs that as the boat made her leisurely way through the ruffled water of the Balkans he was conscious of clouds rolling up on the horizon; 'not only clouds of war, but clouds of private trouble for me; for the American press had become fascinated with my friendship for Wallis, and now pursued us everywhere'. The best description of the cruise of the *Nahlin* is Lady Diana Cooper's in *The Light of Common Day*, because she so clearly perceives the strangeness of the situation. Everyone had a lovely time, but for the King and Wallis it was the end of the beginning.

After meeting Mustapha Kemal in Turkey they took the Orient Express, driven part of the way by the engine-driver Tsar, Boris of Bulgaria.

The King flew home from Zurich while Wallis went on to Paris. Her letters were waiting for her there, and they gave her a shock. Among them were newspaper cuttings from America, and she suddenly realized that she was being discussed the world over. Even Aunt Bessie's letters enclosed cuttings, none of them either accurate or reassuring. When the King telephoned she told him, but he made light of it, pretending to think it was only his Long Island experience over again.

There is no such insulated little world as a yacht, and although they had been acclaimed by crowds, and entertained by the Regent of Jugoslavia, the King of Greece and the dictator of Turkey, Wallis had been out of touch with reality. Once again she had experienced the magic power of the King, to whom everyone deferred and who seemed to be universally loved, yet whose attention was concentrated exclusively upon her. It was the last time she was able to enjoy the extraordinary situation she was living in. Even on board the *Nahlin* she must have wondered how it would all end and what the future could be. The King's love and his strong, obstinate will *seemed* as if they could command and the world would obey, and yet. . . . There were undoubtedly moments when she would have been more than relieved to be able to step down from the impossible pedestal upon which the King had set her.

And now her letters, and the press cuttings, gave her a rough jolt.

# X

# Storm Clouds

A Protestant, if he wants aid or advice on any
matter, can only go to his solicitor.

*Disraeli*

When she got back to London Wallis saw Mr Goddard, her solicitor, about her impending divorce. He had devised a rather foolish plan whereby her petition should be heard at Ipswich, and he had taken a house for her at Felixstowe so that she should be resident within the jurisdiction of the court. If Mr Goddard really believed his little stratagem would work, and that journalists would not be present for the hearing at Ipswich, he was mistaken. It simply made the whole business more noticeable and intriguing than if the divorce had been heard in London in the ordinary way. However, Wallis fell in with his plans, and it is more than possible that he convinced her the whole thing would slip through unnoticed at Ipswich.

Meanwhile the King went up to Balmoral and invited a few friends. Unlike King George v he did not ask the Archbishop of Canterbury, but he had the Marlboroughs, the Buccleuchs and the Roseberys as well as Wallis. Cecil Beaton, who saw a home movie of these guests, noted how the tall, badly or boringly dressed Englishwomen with their untidy hair contrasted with the neat and perfectly turned out Wallis. Once again her name figured in the Court Circular.

The Bryanston Court flat had now been given up, and Wallis took a furnished house in Cumberland Terrace, Regents Park. The King told her of new and disturbing happenings. Mr Baldwin had asked for an audience with him at the Fort. When the Prime Minister returned from his usual protracted holiday, during which he refused even to look at the newspapers, he had found on his desk innumerable press cuttings from America and elsewhere in the world, notably from the Dominions, about Wallis and the King. He told the King he was very worried about the Simpsons' divorce and suggested he might persuade Wallis to withdraw her petition.

96

*Left: Theodore Goddard, the London solicitor who handled Wallis' divorce from Ernest Simpson*

*Below: The King and Wallis entertaining at Balmoral: left to right, the King, Lord Louis Mountbatten, Esmond Harmsworth, Mrs Rogers, Wallis, Mrs Buist, and Lady Louis Mountbatten*

The King indignantly refused. Mr Baldwin also told him that although hitherto the English newspapers had not published the story, before long they were bound to break silence. The King himself had asked two powerful newspaper owners, Lord Beaverbrook and Esmond Harmsworth, to try and arrange for the Ipswich divorce to be reported in a routine way.

Wallis went to Felixstowe with her friends Mr and Mrs George Hunter to wait for her divorce. The hearing was set down for 27 October. The cottage Mr Goddard had taken for her was uncomfortable, the surroundings melancholy in the extreme. When the day came Wallis packed ready to go back to London the moment the proceedings were over. Norman Birkett KC was her counsel; she felt there was deep hostility in the attitude of the judge. However, 'almost reluctantly', as it seemed to her, he granted her a decree *nisi*. Wallis made her way through crowding journalists to her car and left for London.

In those days divorce was still based on ecclesiastical law. Six months had to pass before the divorce could be made absolute, six months of chastity for the petitioner. If he or she could be suspected of having a love affair, or even the opportunity for sexual intercourse could be shown to have existed, the King's Proctor could intervene, the divorce petition would fail and the parties would remain married. This barbarous practice is now a thing of the past, and the best of all grounds for divorce, namely the desire of both parties to a marriage to dissolve it, is no longer 'collusion'. The marriage contract can be terminated without hypocrisy by mutual consent. But as the law then stood it is easy to see that Wallis could have been a target for ill-intentioned hostility.

Early in November Mrs Merryman arrived, and she stayed at Wallis's side throughout the following weeks, the best of chaperons.

The State Opening of Parliament took place on 3 November. *The Times* reported: 'One more page in the history of Parliament has been written. A young King has made his first speech from the Throne. Not alone the fact that his was a Throne by itself, but his whole Royal demeanour made one feel that "in himself was all his state".' His first speech from the Throne was also his last. Harold Nicolson commented on how young he looked, 'like a boy of eighteen', and upon the cockney accent in which he read the Government's speech. On 11 November he laid the traditional wreath of poppies on the Cenotaph, and that night he went down to Portland where he spent two days with the Home Fleet. This was the sort of occasion where all his talents of camaraderie and charm allied to dignity and authority shone at their supreme best.

*Left: Wallis with her aunt, Mrs Merryman, at Fort Belvedere in November 1936*

*Below: Edward VIII, leaving Parliament after the State Opening of 3 November 1936.* The Times *reported that 'his whole Royal demeanour made one feel that "in himself was all his state" '*

None of the sailors, of whatever rank, who saw him then could ever forget the experience.

It was on Friday 13 November, after his return to the Fort where Wallis and Aunt Bessie awaited him, that the King received the famous letter from his Private Secretary Alec Hardinge setting in train the events which culminated in the Abdication. Hardinge warned him that the silence of the press was not going to be maintained much longer, and that when the storm burst the Government might very well resign, and he had 'reason to know' that the King would find it impossible to get anybody to form a new one. The letter ended: 'If Your Majesty will permit me to say so, there is only one step which holds out any prospect of avoiding this dangerous situation, and that is for Mrs Simpson to go abroad *without further delay*, and I would *beg* Your Majesty to give this proposal your earnest consideration before the position has become inevitable. Owing to the changing attitude of the Press the matter has become one of great urgency.'

Upon reading this letter the King sent for Walter Monckton to meet him at Windsor on the Sunday. Monckton was an old friend from Oxford days; he was an eminent lawyer and a man of the world, quite outstanding for his intelligence and extreme niceness. Since 1932 he had been Attorney-General to the Prince of Wales and to the Duchy of Cornwall; they had become close friends. He now asked Monckton to act for him as his personal adviser and liaison with Downing Street in place of Hardinge. 'With a gallantry consistent with his generous spirit he immediately volunteered to serve me' wrote the King in his memoirs. It was obvious that Hardinge must have talked with the Prime Minister before writing his letter, and the King resolved to see Mr Baldwin as soon as possible.

At the Fort he showed Wallis the letter, and he said to her as he had said to Monckton: 'If the Government is opposed to our marriage then I am prepared to go.' This alarmed her, and she implored him not to be impetuous. 'There must be some other way,' she said; but the King answered: 'I don't believe there can be – after this, I cannot leave the challenge hanging in the air another day.'

Wallis wanted to go abroad at once, but this he refused to allow. She tried to show him how hopeless was their position, and that for him to go on fighting could only end in tragedy for him, but he would not listen. Instead he told her he would send for Mr Baldwin and tell him 'that if the country won't approve our marriage, I'm prepared to go'. Wallis went back to Cumberland Terrace. She was really frightened, she felt the trap closing. She says she often reproached herself for not leaving England there and then; she was prevented from doing so by his strong desire that she should stay, and by the near-certainty that if she did go, he would follow. 'Like a doting mallard,' as Shakespeare said of Antony.

According to Harold Nicolson she told Lady Colefax this, and when asked whether the King had suggested marriage Wallis said 'of course not', whereupon Lady Colefax obtained her permission to go and tell Neville Chamberlain this piece of good news. But all the Ministers knew already, from Mr Baldwin, that the King was determined to marry Mrs Simpson. Lady Colefax and Harold Nicolson agreed 'that it is quite possible for the King to have spoken to Baldwin before raising the matter with Wallis herself'. It is worth quoting this just to show how credulous people can become at a moment of crisis, when rumours are flying. Did Lady Colefax really imagine that to her impertinent question Wallis would say 'Yes, I'm to be Queen of the May', for her reply to be retailed all over London? Lady Colefax was a silly person, but Harold Nicolson agreed with her and swallowed the unlikely tale that the King had 'proposed' to Baldwin but not to Wallis.

Meanwhile the King tried to get hold of Lord Beaverbrook, only to discover that he had sailed to America. The King telephoned him and he agreed to turn round and come back on the same ship, the *Bremen*. Much as Beaverbrook liked to spend the winter in the Arizona desert where his chronic asthma disappeared, he liked even better to be where the news was, in the eye of the storm. He also relished the thought of yet one more clash with his old adversary Stanley Baldwin.

The King duly saw the Prime Minister, who told him that he and his senior colleagues were very worried at the prospect of the King's marriage to a divorced lady. He added that whomsoever he married would have to be Queen, and delivered himself of a speech about 'what the people would tolerate and what they would not', just as if he were the Gallup Poll incarnate, as the King wrote years later. The King then said: 'I intend to marry Mrs Simpson as soon as she is free to marry,' and he added that if the Government opposed the marriage he was prepared to go. 'At the mention of the possibility of my leaving the Throne, he was startled.'

That evening the King proposed himself for dinner with his mother in order to tell her of his conversation with the Prime Minister. The idea of his marriage had not hitherto been mentioned between them. With the Queen was the Princess Royal, and 'as I went on and they comprehended that even the alternative of abdication would not deter me from my course, I became conscious

*Stanley Baldwin's 'black beetle' car outside the Fort*

of their growing consternation'. When he asked his mother to allow him to bring Wallis to see her – 'If you were to meet her you would then understand what she means to me, and why I cannot give her up' – Queen Mary refused. She apparently did not tell her son that she had given her word to George v that she would never receive Mrs Simpson, though this is what she told Lady Airlie, (adding: 'He's very much in love with her, poor boy.'). She was also silent about the late King's passionate prayer that the Duke of York should succeed him.

When they parted, Queen Mary wished him well for his forthcoming visit to the South Wales coal-fields.

# XI

# Abdication

Titles are shadows, crowns are empty things;
The good of subjects is the end of Kings.

*Defoe*

Amid all the anxiety connected with his determination to marry whatever the cost, the King went down to South Wales, a two-day tour planned months before. At Brynmawr a long discussion had taken place in the local council as to what they should do to celebrate the King's visit, and it was decided to hang a banner across the road he would take, inscribed: 'We Need Your Help.' It was at Dowlais, at a derelict steelworks, that he spoke the famous words: 'Something must be done.' Photographs of the visit show the white, pinched faces of the men who formed a lane through which he walked. They also show the Minister and other officials who accompanied him trying to box him in as far as they could, but he refused to keep to the official route, determined to see as many people as possible.

He had visited the Rhondda Valley before as Prince of Wales, and what he found most shocking was the intractability of the unemployment problem in the distressed areas. In 1932 he had been there when unemployment nationwide was at its peak of almost three millions. By 1936 the total figure had gone down, but South Wales had not shared in the relative prosperity, mostly concentrated in the Home Counties and the Midlands. What Disraeli called 'the two nations' was no longer only a social division but also to a certain extent a geographical division; there were areas where nobody was employed, everyone was poor and everyone was hungry.

In towns like Brynmawr nothing changed as year followed year. The people had almost lost hope, yet they hung out Union Jacks, put on their tidiest clothes and stood for hours in the cold to see the King. A few years before they had put up a banner: 'Welcome to Our Prince.' Now it was 'We Need Your Help'. His anger on their behalf, his sympathy and understanding of their plight, and the magic of his personality, combined to make him 'a folk legend'.*

*\*The Slump* by John Stevenson and Chris Cook, 1977.

*The King's visit to the coal-fields of South Wales, November 1936. He is talking to unemployed miners at Abertillery*

Nothing that happened afterwards ever altered the love that ordinary people bore King Edward VIII. It was a fact, sometimes awkward, that had to be taken into account every time his future and in particular his place of residence was under discussion.

At the time, the response to his words underlined as hardly anything else could have done his complete impotence. If it gave an added impetus to Mr Baldwin's desire to be rid of him, it also perhaps helped to make him see the futility of his role. If, faced with the terrible, hopeless suffering* of a large segment of his subjects (as they were picturesquely called) he could not even say that something must be done about it, there was very little point in being King. Because, incredible though it may seem, he was criticized for what he had said. His words annoyed the lethargic Mr Baldwin, who never bestirred himself if he could help it; they were words that made headlines in the papers, and they forced the politicians at Westminster, cushioned by their safe Tory majority, to think about a problem they were only too apt to ignore. He himself called what he had said 'the minimum humanitarian response that I could have made to what I had seen': the dingy houses, dismal ruined industry, the white-faced men and women of the Rhondda and Monmouth valleys. The politicians were not inhumane, but they were totally inadequate to their task and had no idea what to do about the situation, and this made them resentful of criticism, even implied criticism.

Back in London the King saw his three brothers one by one and told them of his resolve. Walter Monckton wrote when it was all over that nobody would ever really understand the Abdication who did not realize

> the intensity and depth of the King's devotion to Mrs Simpson. To him she was the perfect woman. She insisted that he should be at his best and do his best at all times, and he regarded her as his inspiration. It is a great mistake to assume that he was merely in love with her in the ordinary physical sense of the term. There was an intellectual companionship and there is no doubt that his lonely nature found in her a spiritual companionship.

He goes on to say that there was a religious side to the problem, the King having strong standards of right and wrong. 'One sometimes felt that the God in whom he believed was a God who dealt him trumps all the time . . . but that view does him less than justice.'

---

*Sir John Boyd Orr in *Food, Health and Income* examined the diets of over 1,000 families and found that the lowest income group of 4½ millions had a diet 'inadequate in all respects'. Seebohm Rowntree found that 49% of all working-class children under the age of five suffered from poverty and were 'living below the minimum'.

He hated the cant and humbug which would have liked to keep him on the Throne with Wallis as his mistress, he hated much of what he saw in the conventional morality.

While the King was in South Wales Esmond Harmsworth invited Wallis to lunch with him at Claridges and made the suggestion that she should marry the King as his morganatic wife. Being an American, she was interested in the idea which was novel to her and which in fact, given the King's chivalrous nature, was probably an almost impossible one. A morganatic wife is a second-class wife, the target of every petty-minded Court official and the recipient of endless pin-pricks. King Edward knew what the position entailed; not only was his own grandfather, Francis of Teck, the child of a morganatic marriage, a fact which but for Queen Victoria's common sense might have ruined the marriage prospects of his mother Queen Mary, but a more recent case was also well known to him. It was that of the heir to the throne of Austria-Hungary, the Archduke Franz Ferdinand. The Emperor Franz Josef had given Countess Sophie Chotek the title of Fürstin Hohenberg, but she had been very much a second-class wife right up to the day when she and her husband, side by side in the carriage at Sarajevo, were both assassinated. Nevertheless the King put the idea to Mr Baldwin, who seized upon it, knowing full well that the Cabinet and the Dominions would turn it down; as a nasty foreign notion it would not go a yard. It is quite a good example of Mr Baldwin's devious methods that he pretended to consider seriously the idea of a morganatic marriage. Lord Beaverbrook, now back in London, saw in a moment that the King had made a tactical error, for he knew as well as Baldwin what the response of the Dominions would be. Yet it was, in fact, the only alternative to abdication.

The King saw various ministers who were friends of his and also Winston Churchill who was out of office. Churchill, Duff Cooper and Beaverbrook all urged delay. They wanted Mrs Simpson to go abroad for the winter, and they wanted the King to be crowned on 12 May and then it would be time to think again. This idea was unacceptable to the King. Coronation is a solemn sacrament, the King is anointed with 'holy oil'; to be crowned, and make a number of vows he was not prepared to keep, was a cynicism of which he was incapable.

All this time Wallis had the almost impossible task of trying to induce him to change his mind and allow her to leave the country and yet not to hurt his feelings at a desperate juncture when he needed her as never before. She knew that nothing could ever be the same again. Either she would lose the King, his wonderful love

*Above: The Prime Minister, Stanley Baldwin, leaving No. 10 Downing Street during the Abdication crisis*

*Below: Lord Beaverbrook. He hoped by his intervention to 'bugger Baldwin'*

for her, the fairy-story life she had been leading during the last two years, or the King would lose his throne. Wallis had no illusions. She did, however, suggest that he might speak on the wireless to the whole nation.

The press storm finally burst after the Bishop of Bradford said at his Diocesan conference on 1 December that he regretted the King had not shown more positive evidence of his awareness of the need for Divine guidance. This was taken to mean guidance as to his marriage, although in his Bradford fastness the Bishop had never heard of Mrs Simpson, or any of the gossip newspaper offices were seething with, and was rather impertinently advocating regular church attendance for the King. Next day the provincial press carried the story, and on 3 December the national newspapers followed. They were their easily predictable selves; *The Times* trying to be statesmanlike, while the *Daily Express* and the *Daily Mail*, reflecting the opinion of their owners, were all for the King. 'The people want their King,' said the *Daily Mail*. The *News Chronicle* had a leader advocating morganatic marriage.

Wallis and her aunt had moved to the Fort, because in London she was stared at every time she left her house; she was also getting anonymous and threatening letters. When she saw her photograph splashed all over the front pages, she tells us she said: 'David, I'm going to leave. I should have gone when you showed me Hardinge's letter. But now nothing you can say will hold me here any longer.' The King did not argue the point this time. He telephoned Lord Brownlow and asked him to take Wallis to France, where Mr and Mrs Herman Rogers invited her to stay with them.

Lord Brownlow lost no time, but why he (or the King) decided they should motor to their destination is a mystery. The obvious way to travel would have been by train; with the blinds drawn newspapermen and photographers would have been thwarted. They were to take the ferry to Dieppe, and on the way Lord Brownlow suggested it might be better after all for them to go to his house, Belton. 'By leaving him to make up his mind alone you will almost certainly bring to pass the conclusion that you and all of us are so anxious to avert.' She asked him what he meant. 'What I'm getting at is simply this,' said Lord Brownlow. 'With you gone the King will not stay in England.' He further told her that the King had confided in him that his mind was made up, that unless the Government gave way he would abdicate. 'Knowing David as I did,' wrote Wallis in her memoirs, 'I was more than doubtful that anyone, including me, could change his mind. If I stayed and my pleas failed, I should always be accused of secretly urging him to give up the Throne.'

# Daily Express

RADIO PROGRAMMES: PAGE 23.

ONE PENNY

THURSDAY, DECEMBER 10, 1936

TODAY'S WEATHER: FOG

NO. 11,411

CABINET SUMMONED IN PREMIER'S ROOM LAST NIGHT:
DEFINITE DECISION TO BE ANNOUNCED TODAY

# ABDICATION IS FEARED

## QUEEN MARY SEES HER SON AT WINDSOR

### Message From Fort Belvedere Read To Cabinet

DOUBLE POLICE FORCE ON DUTY IN LONDON TODAY

### HISTORIC DRAMA IN PARLIAMENT

A COMMUNICATION FROM THE KING WAS READ TO A SPECIAL MEETING OF THE CABINET CALLED SUDDENLY AT THE HOUSE OF COMMONS LAST NIGHT. IT WILL BE ON THE BASIS OF THIS THAT MR. BALDWIN WILL MAKE A DEFINITE AND CONCLUSIVE STATEMENT TO PARLIAMENT ON THE CONSTITUTIONAL ISSUE

DOWNING-STREET FOR
AFTER YESTERDAY'S
MEETING.

Pope's Condition Continues
To Show Improvement.
Hopes To Be Up Today —Page 13

Gas Companies
Millions of Raw
every year

# SUN

24 Pages

2 Cents

DAY, DECEMBER 8, 1936

## ED EDWARD LIKELY TO RENOUNCE MARRIAGE PLANS, IS BELIEF SPREADING THROUGH LONDON

### Willing To Give Up Edward

Mrs. Simpson, throughout the last few weeks, has invariably wished to avoid any action or proposal which might hurt or damage his Majesty or the throne. Today her attitude is unchanged, and she is willing, to withdraw action will solve the problem, to become both situation that has become

### OFFER BY MRS. SIMPSON TO WITHDRAW ISSUED AT CANNES BY AIDE OF

This Fact And Report That Ruler Knew O
ment Before It Was Given Out Strength
Speculation Wedding Is Off

### PRESS PRAISES DIVORCEE
ACTION IN EMPIRE C

Paper Calls It "Her Great Gesture"—C
Backer Of Monarch, Rebuffed In House
Baldwin Is Given Ovation

By PHILIP WAGNER
[London Bureau of The Sun]

London, Dec. 7—The statement from Cannes by M
Warfield Simpson in which she offers "to withdraw forth
situation which has rendered both unhappy and u
will dominate the crisis news in the English papers
morning.

Much is made of the fact that the statement was rea
Brownlow, who not only is an intimate friend of the Kin
is his lord-in-waiting. This strongly indicated that Edw
about the statement before it was made. Few believe Lo
low could have made it, considering his court status, w
King's consent.

### Now Believe Marriage Is Off

Thus for a moment the wild speculation which L
been using for the last few days as a substitute for rea
been around for the time, at least, to a belief that t
his throne, but will choose renun
Baltimorean as a

THE WEATHER

Vol. 54

# King A
Bal
O

PRIME MINISTE
HIS TASK AS
YORK TO R

Monarch's Decision
Premier Tells
Ameri

CORONATION DA
EVERY TIT

Dunkirk,

London,

NO. 11,406

CONSTITUTION

PREMI
AT P

The Duke

M.P.s CHE
BY MR. CH

"No Irrevocal
Statement

SURPRIS
COL.

# THE EVENING SUN

BALTIMORE, THURSDAY, DECEMBER 10, 1936

52 Pages    2 Cents

207,267

## dicates For Mrs. Simpson,
## win Reveals Whole Story
## Two-Month Secret Struggle

### The Lawful Heir

**He said:**

RIBES
NANT",
EORGE VI

And Irrevocable.
Danger Of
Case

EDWARD LOSES
NE TO BE CREATED

P)—The chief of special
said tonight he had re-
guards at the water front
arrival of Edward.

noted Press
ward of England abdicated his

d Simpson as man, not monarch
George, the tall, 40-year-old Duke

After long and anxious consideration, I have determined to renounce the

I am now

Real
have the
the reason
I will
should be
shoulders
stances di
I con
in the for
can no lon
to myself,
ication i
"I, E
ions beyo
irrevocabl
descendan
of abdicat
this tenth
signatures
I dec
have been
ing my fin
But
most injur
and as Kit

# Daily Express

TODAY'S WEATHER: UNSETTLED, COLD.    FRIDAY, DECEMBER 11, 1936

No. 11,412    ONE PENNY

RADIO PROGRAMMES: PAGE 23.

## The King Abdicates: Duke Of York On The
## Baldwin Tells Commons The Whole Sa

### Duke Of York On The

*Edward*

The eighth King Edward of England, who is forty-
two, renounces the Throne and becomes plain Mr.
Windsor. His abdication was announced yesterday in

## GEORGE THE SIX
## To be crowned on May 12—in place of

*Albert*

The Duke of York, who is
Monday and is the second son of
and Queen Mary, will be pr
tomorrow. He will most prob
title King George VI.
**His accession** The new
York Queen and ten-year-old
both the Heir to the Throne
The new Queen her fors
Queen Elizabeth since 1603

THE NEW KING RETURNING TO HIS
PICCADILLY HOME FROM FORT BELVEDERE
JUST BEFORE MIDNIGHT

King 'P
Mrs. Si

Daily Expre

MRS. SIMPSON hea
irrevocable decis
before the world heard.
The telephone con
where Mrs. Simpson i
in-Waiting to the King.
Mrs. King, made
monosyllables, her eyes
for twenty minutes.
"Yes" and "No" w
mon Rogers (Mrs. Simp
and husband heard. W
the receiver, Mrs. Kin
and quietly asked
Every word was unt
the King had spoken
and the decision that
his rapidly, taking a
Later in she told
every word of the Kin
When she returned
little news of the
dramatically the
news of the
Press met and drove

K IN HIS COUNTRY HOME,
HIS THREE BROTHERS—THE
OF GLOUCESTER AND THE
E, KING EDWARD AT TEN
SIGNED THE "INSTRUMENT
WAS READ IN EVERY
H EMPIRE.

t house where, in the words
ied the announcement of his
days of "long and anxious
uchy of Cornwall flying from
the masthead. With a stroke
istian George Andrew Patrick
s and dignities to his brother,
Duke of York, and become

STOP PRESS

HE QUEEN
VISITS
UEEN-TO-BE

RING yesterday's drama
ss Westminster
was sitting alone with
Duchess of York, the
Baldwin told the after-
told the story of where
weeks in the nation's
r, William Berkley's re-
starts on
r, irrevocable first message fo
ment appears in this p
d it came to anyone a
of Mickey's column is
Empire heard the
of a man whose marriage
ormed he pictures on

PORT
makes the
party go
with a
swing!

N.B. Port comes from Portugal ONLY

# ly Express

RADIO PROGRAMMES: PAGE 23.    ONE PENNY

owers; BRIGHT INTERVALS.    FRIDAY, DECEMBER 4, 1936

## RISIS: DRAMATIC NIGHT DEVELOPMENTS
## AND ARCHBISHOP
## CKINGHAM PALACE
### York Has Interview With The King

PLEA
CHILL

" Before
liament

VE BY
WOOD

Beloved"

last night

[Court Circular reproduction]

MARLBOROUGH HOUSE
S.W.1.

Marlborough House
December 3rd.

The King visited Queen Mary today.
The Duke and Duchess of York dined with
Her Majesty this evening.

Reproduction of last night's Court Circular.

## "LONG LIVE THE
## KING"

Five thousand people sang "God Save the King" with
tremendous fervour last night in the Albert Hall at the close of
a demonstration organised by Defence of Freedom and Peace
who joined in the singing were Mr Churchill : Sir
Archibald Sinclair, Sir Archibald Sinclair, 15 members of
... Liberals; and the platform

## MRS. SIMPSON
## READY
## TO GO
## ABROAD

Daily Express Staff Reporter
AT midday yesterday
Mrs Simpson packed
her luggage.
At 7.45 in the evening
the luggage was taken
from her home in Cum-
berland Terrace, Regent's
Park. Her own car, a blue
saloon, was driven to the
front of the house, loaded
with trunks, and driven
away from the front of
the terrace.
Within half an hour

PAGE TWO, COL. ON

### THE KING
The King reached For
Belvedere just before
to be expected at th
Palace before noon.

THE TEST
ENGLAND COLLAPSE
England won the toss
first Test match at Bri
bane today and batted first
Washington was for fir
"Buck" Laird for th
Hammond & Robinson
McCormick &

UDEX

New King Is H
By Cheering C

MIDNIGHT VISIT TO

WHEN the new King retu
Belvedere to his home in
last night he was greeted by
which completely blocked the
in the forecourt cheer afte
there were shouts of "We wan
Men in evening dress
pressed their faces to the
were rewarded with a friend
After the new King
to the crowd and raised hi

After he had gone into
anxieties of the last few hour
loosened as the crowd tall
While their prayers tall
had been answered, and the
had knowledge that the K
At ten minutes
his mother at Marlbo
he left

QUEEN MARY GOES OUT

Queen Mary drove to Sydenham
afternoon in the rain and st
afterwards she went back
drove along the parade and back
down Anerley Hill
returned to Marl

*Wallis with her detective, Inspector Evans, leaving the Hôtel de la Poste in Rouen, during her nightmare dash across France to sanctuary at Lou Viei, chased by the press of the world*

They drove on to Newhaven, discussing how they could persuade the King 'to give up the idea of marriage and thus end the crisis'. They had the King's driver, Ladbroke, and Inspector Evans, an experienced detective, with them, and their dash across France in Wallis's Buick was a nightmare. They had left the Fort on 3 December; not until early morning on the 6th did they reach the Villa Lou Viei near Cannes. In those days there were no motorways, they were obliged to go through innumerable towns and villages. Reporters lay in wait for them at every turn.

Wherever they stopped, Wallis telephoned the King. Anyone who used the French telephone for long-distance calls in the thirties can picture the misery of it. The lines were hopelessly bad, he only seemed to hear half of what she was trying to tell him, imploring him to stand firm. She had to shout, so that Lord Brownlow was afraid the reporters would hear, and at the other end of the line, according to Walter Monckton who was now living at the Fort, the King had to shout so that the entire household heard what he was saying. The British Secret Service listened in to these hectic and frustrating dialogues, and the click of the listener-in was constantly heard, a very tiresome sound because it gives the illusion that the communication is about to be cut off. After lunch at Evreux, Wallis left the notes she had made for her telephone call behind, but there was nothing to be done, they had to press on.

They slept at Blois, leaving the hotel at 3 a.m. in order to evade the reporters, but in Lyons they had to stop and ask the way. Wallis was instantly recognized by a passer-by who cried out: 'Voila la dame!' Before a crowd could gather Ladbroke drove on.

Followed by the press of the world they stopped at Vienne for luncheon at the Restaurant de la Pyramide. The owner, Madame Point, knew Wallis, and seeing how exhausted she looked took her to her own room. While the crowd of reporters were guzzling the fare provided in this temple of gastronomy, Mme Point helped Wallis to climb through a lavatory window into an alley where the car was waiting. Those who know Mme Point and her comfortable kindness can well imagine how the tired and harrassed Wallis must have welcomed her aid.

They raced on through sleet and snow, and at 2 a.m. reached Lou Viei. There was nevertheless a crowd waiting outside the gate, but Wallis crouched on the floor and Lord Brownlow threw a rug over her as they dashed into the courtyard. Wallis was safely with her friends.

The whole of this December journey was mismanaged, particularly so in the way Lord Brownlow dealt with the newspapermen. As a rule they behave fairly if they are treated fairly. Here was perhaps the biggest newspaper story of all time, and nothing was going to stop them one and all trying for a scoop. Wallis, who had nothing to hide, should have spoken to them at Vienne or before, saying that she was going to stay with friends and that was all. If she could not bring herself to see them, Lord Brownlow should have spoken to them on her behalf. There was no point in throwing a rug over her since they knew she was there. No great harm was done, but the journey was unnecessarily exhausting; there was no need for them to behave like fugitives from a chain gang.

# XII

# King into Duke

Prince, Prince-Elective on the modern plan,
Fulfilling such a lot of people's Wills,
You take the Chiltern Hundreds while you can;
A storm is coming on the Chiltern Hills.

*G. K. Chesterton*

Meanwhile in England everything was speeding towards the inevitable end. The King worked on his wireless speech, but when Mr Baldwin saw a draft of what he proposed to say it was promptly vetoed. 'Neither Mrs Simpson nor I have ever sought to insist that she should be queen. All we desired was that our married happiness should carry with it a proper title and dignity for her, befitting my wife,' wrote the King. Baldwin considered that this proposition had already been adequately dealt with when the Cabinet and the Dominions unanimously rejected morganatic marriage.

By now, Mr Baldwin hoped the King would abdicate. He said so once, showing, as the French say, 'the tip of his ear': 'Only time I was frightened, because I thought he might change his mind.' Mr Baldwin was somebody it was very easy to dislike. As a politician he presided over the beginning of England's long decline; as a man he was unattractive, with unpleasant habits, always scratching himself, 'blinking, stuffy, neurotic'.* But it is unfair to blame him for the Abdication. The plain fact is that nobody could envisage a King married to a lady with two ex-husbands living. However, when he said in the House that the Government was not prepared to introduce legislation to make a morganatic marriage possible, and that the Dominions agreed, Churchill shouted at him: 'You won't be satisfied until you've broken him, will you?'

On the 7 December Baldwin made a statement to the House of Commons, Churchill intervened and was shouted down. The King's great friend, Lloyd George, was not in the House; he had gone to the West Indies and could not get back in time to be present.

*Harold Nicolson.

He sent a cable to his son Gwilym and his daughter Megan, both of whom were Members of Parliament:

> Hope you are not going to join the Mrs Grundy harriers who are hunting the King from the Throne. It is for the nation to choose its Queen, but the King cannot be denied the right of humblest citizen to choose his own wife. Had he not decided to marry the lady not a word would have been said by the Scribes and Pharisees. Had King not as prince and sovereign exposed continued neglect by Government of chronic distress, poverty and bad housing conditions amongst people in his realm, convinced they would not have shown such alacrity to dethrone him. You may make any use you like of this telegram. Lloyd George.

Lloyd George was right about the Scribes and Pharisees. Victor Cazalet* afterwards noted in his diary 'Stanley Baldwin said he quite appreciated that a King might indulge in a little quiet whoring'. A. J. Sylvester, Lloyd George's secretary, wrote: 'Churchill was howled down when he pleaded for delay before a final decision was reached and the episode did him substantial political damage. However, Lloyd George and Churchill working together for the King would have been a far more formidable proposition, and there were many on Baldwin's side who were relieved that Lloyd George was out of the way.' Had he been there, MPs would not have had such an easy task brushing Churchill aside. These two, though they were at odds with the Government, were far and away the greatest personalities in that Parliament. Nothing would have been changed, however, because the King was determined not to countenance a 'King's party' or any action that would divide the nation. He wished to hand over to the Duke of York in such a way that the monarchy as an institution was untouched by his decision to go.

On Tuesday 8 December the King's brothers assembled at the Fort for dinner together with Mr Baldwin and Sir Edward Peacock. The King was so exhausted by the tensions and stresses of the last days that Monckton advised him to dine in his room. However, he came down, sat at the head of the table, played the perfect host, and was the only person present, according to Walter Monckton, who was not as white as a sheet, 'This dinner party was, I think, his *tour de force*.' The Duke of York said: 'Look at him! We simply cannot let him go.'

Earlier that day, in the villa still besieged by hopeful pressmen, Wallis, helped by Lord Brownlow and Herman Rogers, wrote out

*Victor Cazalet, a Tory MP, was a great personal friend of the Baldwins. He was a Christian Scientist and teetotaller.

*Right: Walter Monckton, the King's adviser, at No. 10 Downing Street in December 1936*

*Below: Lord Brownlow, Katherine Rogers, Wallis, and Herman Rogers outside the Villa Lou Viei in Cannes*

a statement. Intensely unhappy and worried, her one idea was to stop the King abdicating. At the same time she must not seem to be deserting him at such a stressful moment. She said: 'Mrs Simpson throughout the last few weeks has invariably wished to avoid any action or proposal which would hurt or damage His Majesty or the Throne. Today her attitude is unchanged, and she is willing, if such action would solve the problem, to withdraw from a situation that has been rendered both unhappy and untenable.'

She read it to the King on the telephone. All he said, after a long silence, was: 'Go ahead, if you wish; it won't make any difference.' Lord Brownlow gave the statement to the press; Wallis says a terrible weight lifted from her mind.

Next day the King telephoned to tell her that Mr Goddard the solicitor was on his way to see her. 'Baldwin is behind it' said the King. 'Don't be influenced by anything Goddard says.' Very late that night Inspector Evans brought Lord Brownlow a note signed by four British newspaper correspondents: 'Mr Goddard, the well-known lawyer who acts for Mrs Simpson, has arrived at Marseilles by special plane. He brought with him Dr Kirkwood, the well-known gynaecologist and his anaesthetist.' Wallis writes: 'I was shocked to the core of my being. Gynaecologist? Anaesthetist? Somebody had obviously gone mad.'

Mr Goddard arrived early on the Wednesday morning, having motored from Marseilles. He found a furious Lord Brownlow, asking angrily for the explanation of his strange conduct. The answer was that Goddard had a weak heart and his doctor had insisted on coming with him on the aeroplane. The 'anaesthetist' was simply Mr Goddard's clerk. His doctor, Kirkwood, was a general practitioner, but he had over the years delivered so many babies that he had acquired quite a reputation in fashionable circles as a gynaecologist on the side. For sheer spite, the way Goddard's journey was reported and the roles ascribed to his companions would take a lot of beating.

Having apologized for the absurd story, for which he was not to blame, Mr Goddard proceeded to give the reason for his visit. He asked Mrs Simpson to withdraw her divorce petition. She called in Lord Brownlow, who said: 'If the King does abdicate his object will be marriage, and for you to scrap your divorce will produce an all-round tragedy.' Nevertheless Wallis telephoned the Fort and told the King she had arranged with Mr Goddard to withdraw her divorce petition. 'There was a long silence. Then with emotion David answered that matters had already gone much further than I realized.' He made George Allen speak to her; the King was in the process of abdicating, she was told. When she repeated this to Mr Goddard he took his departure from the villa and from the history books. His interventions had never been happy, they ended (with the 'gynaecologist' and the 'anaesthetist') in pure farce; but for Wallis it was far from comic.

She was in despair, and when Lord Brownlow suggested she should leave Europe she began to make arrangements to board a ship at Genoa; then, having rehearsed what she was going to say, she made one more effort of renunciation, one more 'dreadful ordeal of breaking the news to David' on the telephone, but this time he cut her short. 'I can't seem to make you understand the position. It's all over. The instrument of Abdication is already prepared. The only conditions on which I can stay here are if I renounce you for all time. And this, of course, I will not do.' He said he had given the Cabinet the final word. Wallis was crying when the conversation ended. 'I was conscious only of having failed tragically.'

At the villa they listened to the King's farewell broadcast. Wallis lay on a sofa 'With my hands over my eyes to hide my tears'.

When Mr Baldwin addressed the House of Commons he told the whole story. He had been asked by the King to mention two things, firstly that the King had entire confidence in his brother as successor, and secondly that 'the other person most intimately concerned' had consistently tried, to the last, to dissuade him from the decision he had taken. Characteristically, Mr Baldwin made the first point about the Duke of York and omitted the second about Mrs Simpson. Walter Monckton says this was 'a little hard' on Wallis. The omission made the ex-King angry, and from that moment dated his, very natural, dislike of Mr Baldwin.

Next day he was at last permitted to broadcast to the nation; the whole world listened. He had written his speech with Walter Monckton's help, and Winston Churchill had come down to the Fort, as he constantly did during those days, and added a few touches. Queen Mary did her best to dissuade him. 'Don't you think,' she wrote to him 'that as he [the Prime Minister] has said everything that could be said . . . it will not now be necessary for you to broadcast this evening . . . you might spare yourself this extra strain and emotion. Do please take my advice.' But as we have seen, the Prime Minister had not said everything that could be said, and now the former King seized his opportunity.

The head of the BBC, Sir John Reith, introduced 'His Royal Highness, Prince Edward' and then left him alone with Walter Monckton and the microphone in a little room in Windsor Castle.

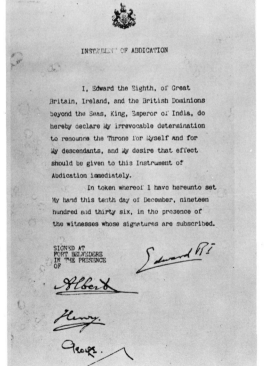

*Above: The farewell broadcast, Windsor Castle*

*Left: The Instrument of Abdication signed by Edward in the presence of his three brothers: Albert, Duke of York, Henry, Duke of Gloucester, and George, Duke of Kent*

*Below: Edward, now to be Duke of Windsor, leaving Windsor Castle after making his Abdication speech*

At long last I am able to say a few words of my own. I have never wanted to withhold anything, but until now it has not been constitutionally possible for me to speak. A few hours ago I discharged my last duty as King and Emperor, and now that I have been succeeded by my brother the Duke of York my first words must be to declare my allegiance to him. This I do with all my heart. You all know the reasons which have impelled me to renounce the Throne, but I want you to understand that in making up my mind I did not forget the Country or the Empire, which as Prince of Wales and lately as King, I have for twenty-five years tried to serve. But you must believe me when I tell you that I have found it impossible to carry the heavy burden of responsibility and to discharge my duties as King as I would wish to do without the help and support of the woman I love. And I want you to know that the decision I have made has been mine, and mine alone. This was a thing I had to judge for myself. The other person most nearly concerned has tried, up to the last, to persuade me to take a different course. I have made this, the most serious decision of my life, only upon a single thought of what would in the end be best for all. This decision has been made less difficult for me by the sure knowledge that my brother, with his long training in the public affairs of this country and with his fine qualities, will be able to take my place forthwith without interruption or injury to the life and progress of the Empire. And he has one matchless blessing, enjoyed by so many of you, and not bestowed on me, a happy home with his wife and children.

During these hard days I have been comforted by my Mother and by my family.

The Ministers of the Crown, and in particular Mr Baldwin the Prime Minister, have always treated me with full consideration. There has never been any constitutional difference between me and them and between me and Parliament. Bred in the constitutional tradition by my Father, I should never have allowed any such issue to arise.

Ever since I was Prince of Wales, and later on when I occupied the Throne, I have been treated with the greatest kindness by all classes wherever I have lived or journeyed through the Empire. For that I am very grateful.

I now quit altogether public affairs, and I lay down my burden. It may be some time before I return to my native land, but I shall always follow the fortunes of the British race and Empire with profound interest, and if, at any time in the future, I can be found of service to His Majesty in a private station, I shall not fail.

And now we all have a new King.

I wish him and you, his people, happiness and prosperity with all my heart.

God bless you all.

God save the King.

This speech, and the idiosyncratic voice, had a strangely moving impact upon the millions who heard it; a brilliant, unforgettable performance.

After the broadcast, Prince Edward, now created Duke of Windsor by King George VI, went to Royal Lodge to take leave of his family, and then he and Walter Monckton motored to Portsmouth. Admiral Sir William Fisher bade him farewell for the Navy with tears in his eyes. He sailed for France in *HMS Fury* accompanied by Major Ulick Alexander and his great friend 'Joey', Captain Piers Legh; his destination was Schloss Enzesfeld in Austria where he was to stay with Baron Eugen Rothschild.

When the hurly-burly was done, Lord Beaverbrook was asked why, since he thought little of the monarchy and had never been a friend of the Monarch, he had decided to come back from America. He answered laconically: 'To bugger Baldwin.'* His idea had been that what Churchill used to call the 'goody-goodies' would resign and that a new administration led by Churchill and composed of 'King's men', himself included, would then be formed. Even among those (and they were not few in number) who heartily disliked and despised Mr Baldwin, this would not have been considered a proper course.** It would have divided Parliament and divided the country and most likely have wrecked the monarchy. Beaverbrook cared nothing for the monarchy; he was disappointed that 'our cock won't fight' as he said of the King. It was the King's unflinching resolve not to allow any such fight on his behalf that made the transition perfectly smooth and easy. When he finally took leave of him Winston Churchill quoted the lines:

> He nothing common did or mean
> Upon that memorable scene.

On Sunday, 13 December Cosmo Lang, the Archbishop of Canterbury, broadcast a sermon castigating the former King and the King's friends. Lord Birkenhead in his biography of Walter Monckton wrote: 'There were no excuses for this lapse. The King had gone, as Walter Monckton said, like a great gentleman, refusing to be made the pretext for any action which might have

*Lord Beaverbrook's biographer, Tom Driberg, points out how he failed in this endeavour.

**Churchill, though in private he referred to Baldwin as 'a contemptible figure', would never have joined Beaverbrook in such an enterprise.

*'My Lord Archbishop, what a scold you are': Cosmo Lang, Archbishop of Canterbury*

endangered the State.' Most people condemned the Archbishop, and a lampoon gave much pleasure:

My lord Archbishop, what a scold you are
And when your man is down, how bold you are
Of Christian charity how scant you are
Oh! Old Lang Swine! How full of Cantuar!

The Archbishop of York also attacked the Duke of Windsor, but nobody paid much attention to him. It was Cosmo Lang who bore the obloquy.

English hypocrisy, a national failing, was in evidence throughout the Abdication crisis. It was a dreadful disappointment to Mr Baldwin that the King never seemed to wrestle with himself. Baldwin had looked forward to a dark night of the soul, even when the outcome was decided. He felt cheated. 'The King never went through Hell' he told Victor Cazalet, who also quotes in his diary a letter from 'a close friend of the royal family': 'I don't think we could ever imagine a more incredible tragedy, and the agony of it all has been beyond words. And the melancholy fact remains still at the present moment that he for whom we agonized is the one person it did not touch. Poor soul, a fearful awakening is awaiting his completely blinded reason before very long.' This lady (we are not told the sex of the writer, but it is safe to assume it was a lady) went on: 'I don't think you need feel the Archbishop failed to express the right thing.'

Leaving aside the oddly exaggerated style, it is the conviction that the Duke would soon be unhappy which is so striking. His continued happiness, year after year, must deeply have disappointed the ungenerous 'close friend of the royal family', who had so confidently and gleefully counted upon a 'fearful awakening'.

# XIII

# *Marriage*

For winter's rains and ruins are over
And all the season of snows and sins,
The days dividing lover and lover
The light that loses, the night that wins;
And time remembered is grief forgotten
And frosts are slain and flowers begotten,
And in green underwood and cover
Blossom by blossom the spring begins.

*Swinburne*

A few days after he arrived in Austria the Duke was joined
by Lord Brownlow who brought letters from Wallis. (He
later described the Duke's room, with sixteen photographs
of Wallis in it.) Walter Monckton considered it was essential that
they live in different countries until her divorce was made absolute,
because it was rumoured that certain malignant persons still hoped
to prevent the marriage for which the Duke had given up his
crown. When the Duke of Westminster invited him to stay in
Normandy even that was judged to be too near Cannes.

On Boxing Day a letter signed 'A Londoner' was printed in the
*New York Times:*

> Let the American people despise us, if they must, that we did
> not smash windows, lynch politicians and bring down in ruins
> the whole structure which our ancestors had so laboriously
> built up; but let not the foul lie be spread that we approved
> and applauded the disgraceful manoeuvre by which powerful
> interests removed from public life one of the most courageous,
> sincere and straightforward of living Englishmen . . .

In their sorrow at the loss of a beloved King, many people came to
believe in a 'hidden hand' which, in fact, did not exist.

The early months of 1937 were extremely frustrating for the
Duke, who, formerly so busy and active, now had nothing much to
do, except to go skiing when the weather was right, a guest in
somebody else's house, parted from the only person he wished to
be with, and looking forward to telephone conversations each
evening which were usually more annoying than comforting, with
bad lines and frequent cuts.

The Duke's old friend and equerry, Major 'Fruity' Metcalfe,
joined him in Austria, but it cannot be said that the presence of
this former boon companion afforded much pleasure to either of

*Major 'Fruity' Metcalfe, the Duke's old friend and equerry, was his chosen companion for the weeks of waiting in Austria. To his wife, Lady Alexandra, he wrote letters complaining of his lot*

them. Metcalfe wrote letters to his wife in which he rather often complained of his lot, though sometimes he admired the Duke, as, for example, when he went to a party at the British Legation in Vienna. There was music, something he could hardly bear, yet he pretended to enjoy every moment 'and was wonderful as he always is when he really tries'. The grumbles were about the Duke's alleged stinginess.

No doubt, like many rich people, he was sometimes forgetful; royal persons are unaccustomed to handling money. Probably he would have been more careful if he had thought the Metcalfes were poor. With Bruce Ogilvy, for example, a penniless second son, he was the reverse of stingy. Ogilvy writes: 'He was said to be mean about money; I can only say that I never found him so. . . . When I left him, full of debts, he offered to pay them. He also gave me a substantial cheque for a wedding present.' He adds that he did not allow the Prince (as he then was) to pay his debts, and 'he certainly became mean in later life and I think Wallis's influence had a lot to do with that'. Like many, though not all, of the Duke's old friends, Bruce Ogilvy did not like Wallis, the interloper who changed and spoilt everything from their point of view, and this is easily understood. But the notion that in after years the Duke, encouraged by the Duchess, was mean about money will strike those who knew him as a generous host as wide of the mark. It was well known in France that no charity approached the Windsors for money in vain. In any case there was no Wallis to urge meanness at Enzesfeld, so that she cannot be blamed for Metcalfe's miseries.

While he was in Austria the Duke of Windsor often telephoned his brother, the new King, rather naturally thinking it might help to discuss this and that with his newly-installed successor. Apparently these telephone conversations upset George VI; he felt obliged to get Walter Monckton to ask the Duke to stop ringing him up, an episode which helps to explain his attitude in 1939. The Duke was simply surprised, and of course did as he was asked; he probably never realized the effect his strong personality had upon his brothers.

Meanwhile at Lou Viei Wallis was having a wretched time. The army of reporters outside the gate soon melted away, so that she felt free to go for walks. But every morning with her breakfast tray-loads of letters appeared, many of them anonymous, most of them hostile, some of them threatening her life. She says the most abusive came from Canadians, and Americans of British birth. Although there were quite a few friendly letters, including one from Ernest Simpson, she became obsessed with the notion that a calculated effort to discredit and destroy her was being made. Herman

Rogers gave her excellent advice: 'You've got to learn to rise above all this. Put it out of your mind.'

Easy to say, hard to do, but by degrees Wallis did put it out of her mind. She became immune, just as everyone in the public eye has to become immune. She learnt, as famous people must, to obey her own conscience and pay no attention to attacks or spite from outside.

Mr Baldwin had complained that during the Abdication crisis the King 'never went through Hell'. As we know on the best authority, hell has more than one circle, and it is probable that before she succeeded in taking Mr Rogers' advice Wallis did go through some sort of hell. No very powerful imagination is needed to see the situation from her point of view. Almost overnight she found herself, from having been the loved and envied, cast as a wily, black villainess. Then she must have asked herself over and over again whether she could live up to the image of her that the King carried in his heart. Could she continue to be the perfect woman, the inspiration, the heroine of this very unusual man who needed her so desperately that he had given up his throne? He had endured a chorus of advice from his ministers, his friends, his brothers, his mother, brushing it aside as if it were not of the slightest consequence or as if he simply failed to hear; but would not echoes of it remain to torment them both?

He was not an infatuated boy of eighteen but a man of forty-two whom she had known for six years, during which he had become ever more devoted to her. She certainly loved him too, but the very last thing she had wanted was for him to make enormous sacrifices for her, thus placing upon her a burden too heavy to be borne. She had wanted a divorce for Ernest Simpson's sake; he had begun to look very foolish and he had found an ideal wife in his and her old friend Mary Kirk Raffray. But Wallis had emphatically not wanted to marry the King of England, or to be the cause of his abdication. Given the overwhelming nature of his devotion, only a monster of vanity and obtuseness could have surveyed the future without fear. Wallis was neither vain nor obtuse. Also, in addition to his love, there was nearly everyone else's hatred and malice to be contended with.

As time went on she began to recover from these depressing thoughts. She was resilient, and no doubt friends helped her, particularly Herman and Katherine Rogers with their affection, tact and generosity, but there were others. Osbert Sitwell's poem 'Rat Week', in which he pretends that no sooner had the King abdicated than all his friends and Wallis's deserted them, denying ever having known *her*, is rather spiteful and completely untrue.

One of the 'rats', described by Sitwell as 'Colefax in her iron cage of curls', happened to be on the Riviera and hurried to see Wallis, while the few people she knew with houses in the neighbourhood – Somerset Maugham, Daisy Fellowes – immediately invited her. Nobody had been intimidated by the Archbishop's attack on the King's friends; most of the friends laughed, some (like Walter Monckton) were angry. Wallis was depressed and anxious for obvious reasons, but she was never deserted by her friends.

At that time, and for the rest of her life, people who had once or twice found themselves in her proximity were apt to dine out for ever on the subject of her shortcomings while her friends were ignored when they spoke of her qualities. She most likely never knew this. She knew she had a 'bad press'; the newspapers always enjoyed publishing disagreeable tittle-tattle, and unbecoming photographs of the Windsors, but people she met were all 'smarmy as be damned' as the Duke once put it. This is one of the advantages, or disadvantages, that royal personages live with. It makes it fairly difficult for them to distinguish the true from the false.

The dreary months passed, spring came and Wallis began to prepare for her wedding. Both the Duke and the new King thought it would be a bad idea for the marriage to take place on the Côte d'Azur which sounded frivolous and flighty. They were determined to marry in France, because the French have strict laws about the privacy of individuals which would protect them from sightseers and journalists. When a French-American, Charles Bedaux, offered to lend his château in Touraine it sounded ideal and they accepted. The Château de Candé was hidden in a park, a big, comfortable old castle recently restored. Wallis motored there with the Rogers early in March; she was delighted with it. Candé had much to recommend it, sitting in the middle of its park it would be a simple matter to keep the hordes well away.

A few old friends came from Paris to see her from time to time, among them Mrs Rex Benson, an American who lived in London. They had a long talk and Leslie Benson remembers Wallis saying: 'You know, I never wanted this marriage.'* She was certainly speaking the truth, and it is worth quoting since even now she is sometimes portrayed as an adventuress who with her wiles lured the King of England from his throne. During these months of waiting she made up her mind that as far as lay in her power she would make the Duke happy, it would be her life's work from now on. As we shall see, she succeeded to an almost miraculous extent.

In England the year before the King had given Wallis a cairn terrier called Slipper. When she dashed away to France with Lord

*In conversation with the author.

129

*Château de Candé, the home of Charles Bedaux, which he offered to Wallis and the Duke of Windsor for their wedding*

*Wallis and Katherine Rogers at Candé with the Cairn terrier, Slipper, which was killed by an adder*

*Left: Wallis and the Duke reunited at last at Candé, May 1937*

*Above: The wedding of Wallis and the Duke of Windsor at Candé, 3 June 1937*
*The Duke and Duchess posing for the photographers with Herman Rogers (left) and Major Metcalfe (right)*

On the balcony steps at Candé: left to right, Aunt Bessie, the Rev. Anderson Jardine, who performed the wedding ceremony, Wallis, the Duke of Windsor, Randolph Churchill

The wedding breakfast with Walter Monckton (centre) and Major Metcalfe (right). Flowers were arranged by Constance Spry

*Rev. Anderson Jardine's prayerbook, autographed after the wedding ceremony by the Duke and Duchess*

Brownlow she left Slipper behind at the Fort, and he went with the Duke of Windsor to Enzesfeld. During the waiting time at Candé Slipper was sent to keep her company. One day, chasing a rabbit into the wood, he was bitten by a viper and died. Wallis was inconsolable; the cairn's death shed deep gloom for many days.

On 3 May George Allen telephoned from London to tell Wallis that her divorce was now absolute and she rang up the Duke to tell him the good news. 'Wallis,' he said, 'the Orient Express passes through Salzburg this afternoon. I shall be at Candé in the morning.' And so he was, accompanied by his equerry, Dudley Forwood. He rushed up the castle steps two at a time: 'Darling, it's been so long! I can hardly believe this is you, and I am here!'

They decided to be married after the coronation, for which the date of 12 May had been retained; as it was on the coronation mugs it had seemed easier to keep to it. They all listened to the ceremony on the wireless in the Candé drawing room.

Wallis was superstitious and did not want a May wedding so they fixed it for 3 June. She had ordered a blue crêpe satin dress from Mainbocher with a hat to match from Reboux. Constance Spry, who was devoted to the bride, came from England to arrange the flowers, and Cecil Beaton to photograph the couple on the wedding eve. He remembers the scent of lilies and white peonies in the castle. The only French journalist who was present at the wedding was Maurice Schumann, who years later was many times a Minister and is a member of the Académie Française. He says that on her wedding day Wallis woke to a 'Wallis blue sky'. He praises the elegance of the Duchess and what he calls 'her very great dignity'.*

A few friends came, including Major Metcalfe as best man, Lady Alexandra Metcalfe, Hugh Lloyd-Thomas, Lady Selby, Randolph Churchill and others, but none of the Duke's relations.

'Alas! the wedding day in France of David to Mrs Warfield. . . . We all telegraphed to him' wrote Queen Mary in her diary.

A Church of England clergyman, braving his bishop's ban, had volunteered to conduct the marriage service, which seems to have pleased the Duke who wanted a religious ceremony. The legions of the press gathered at nearby Tours; Herman Rogers, by now accustomed to the job, acted as liaison with them. Although he was disappointed that his brother the Duke of Kent had not come, for the Duke everything was joy and happiness until the unfortunate Walter Monckton appeared, the bearer of evil tidings, a letter from the King. This letter said that the King was advised by the British and Dominions Prime Ministers that when the Duke

*In conversation with the author.

136

*The world press at the gates of the Château*

renounced the Throne he had also given up his royal titles, including the right to the title of Royal Highness. The King was now re-creating him a Royal Highness, but the title did not extend to the Duke's wife. In conclusion, the King hoped that this painful decision he had been forced to take would not be considered an 'insult' by the Duke. It goes without saying that the painful decision *was* considered an insult, a deadly insult. The Duchess writes :'The letter enraged David. He exclaimed: "I know Bertie – I know he couldn't have written this letter on his own. Why in God's name would they do this to me at this time!" ' To Walter Monckton he said: 'This is a nice wedding present!'

Characteristically, the Duchess of Windsor did not mind for herself, though she did for the Duke. She never gave a fig for titles and would have been perfectly content, had it not been for the Duke's violent reaction. A morganatic marriage had never been an ideal solution in his eyes because it made Wallis a second-class wife. He had accepted it as the only alternative to renouncing his throne, but it had been rejected unanimously by the British Cabinet and the Dominions. Now that he had abdicated in order to marry, here he was with a morganatic marriage after all.

In fact it was a clever move on the part of the politicians who devised it. They knew, none better, that the Duke was loved in a quite special way in Britain. He was 'a folk legend' and legends do not disappear at the wave of a wand. They dreaded his return to his native land, and they reckoned, quite correctly, that he would never come back unless his wife was treated properly. In order to ensure his continued absence they acted illegally, in the opinion of learned lawyers. Sir William Jowitt, a future Lord Chancellor, so advised the Duke. (The editor of *Burke's Peerage* wrote years later that it was 'the most flagrant act of discrimination in the whole history of our dynasty'.) Walter Monckton* said that nothing and nobody could take away the Duke's title, as son of a sovereign, of Royal Highness, and that since he was married according to the law of the land his wife automatically became a Royal Highness too. Monckton said that if the Duke had brought an action in the English courts to establish the Duchess's right to be a Royal Highness he would have won it, but this of course was something he would never do.

Everything she possibly could to make their wedding a perfect day for the Duke, Wallis had done. The quiet country setting, the rooms full of flowers, the food, all were perfection. The yawning gaps among the guests, the fact that the ever-faithful Aunt Bessie was the only relation present, were not her fault.

*In conversation with the author.

After the wedding breakfast the guests were received one by one by the Duke and Duchess, and for the first time the problem arose of who was going to bow or curtsy to the Duchess as they did to the Duke. This recurred for the rest of their lives, and it was noticeable that everyone with the slightest pretension to good manners treated her, for the Duke's sake, as he would have wished. Only people very anxious and unsure of themselves, hoping, perhaps, to show they knew what was what, did otherwise.

Afterwards Walter Monckton took the Duchess aside; he 'told her that most people in England disliked her very much because the Duke had married her and given up his throne, but that if she kept him happy all his days that would change, but that if he were unhappy nothing would be too bad for her.' The Duchess said: 'Walter, don't you think I have thought of all that? I think I can make him happy.'

Fate had given her a tremendous challenge; it was not of her choosing, but she was determined to meet it.

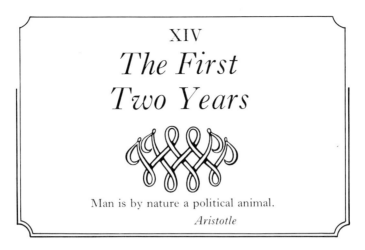

# XIV

# The First Two Years

Man is by nature a political animal.

*Aristotle*

After a honeymoon in Austria at Wasserleonburg, an old castle belonging to Count Paul Munster whose wife Peggy was a cousin of the Duke's friend Lord Dudley, the Windsors went to Paris. Probably the first year was the most difficult of all their married life. During the Abdication crisis the then Duke of York had told Walter Monckton that the Duke of Windsor could, after an interval, come back and live at Fort Belvedere, the house and garden to which he was so deeply attached, but as the months went on it became obvious that this was a promise he was not going to be allowed to keep. Yet the Duke could not bring himself to believe that his present circumstances were to be permanent. When, according to the best legal advice, he discovered that the blow he had received on his wedding day was of doubtful legality he felt convinced that before long it would be admitted that his wife was indeed a Royal Highness. Then they could go back to the Fort, and he could take on some of the work of the royal family. For this reason he did not buy a house, and in a rented house neither gardening nor anything else seems worth while. Sir Dudley Forwood, who was with the Windsors during this testing time, writes: 'During my tours of duty with them both, she showed every kindness and understanding; indeed often, when His Royal Highness was being somewhat difficult, she would overcome his stubbornness.'* In Sir Dudley's opinion, the Duchess has never been given a 'fair deal'.

During their stay at the Hôtel Meurice the new Prime Minister, Neville Chamberlain, called on the Duke. They had a long talk, and he promised to ask the Palace when the Windsors could go home. Nothing happened, and a few months later the Duke asked again. The Palace and Downing Street played a sort of game with

*In a letter to the author.

*Previous page: The Duke and Duchess on their honeymoon at Wasserleonburg*

*Top: Wasserleonburg Castle, the home of Count Paul Munster*

*Above: A lunch party at Wasserleonburg, June 1937. Left to right: Wallis, Colin Buist (equerry to the Duke of York), Walter Monckton, Dudley Forwood, Mrs Buist, Foxie Gwynne (later Countess of Sefton)*

him, each putting the blame for delay upon the other, turn and turn about. Perhaps neither wished to incur the odium of telling him outright that the Duchess was never to be a Royal Highness, and that the reason was they emphatically did not want a living 'folk legend' to come back to England and had hit upon this simple way of stopping him. The rather cowardly evasions were exasperating to the Duke, who had he been placed in like circumstances would have made it a point of honour to be perfectly frank and truthful.

The Duchess found a furnished house at Versailles where they stayed for a few months, and then they took a lease of the Château de la Croë at Cap d'Antibes on the sea. The Duke liked the South of France; what he never liked was living for more than a short time in a town. He looked upon his present life in France as an interlude, it never occurred to him that he would not be back in England before very long.

He was a modest man, and he probably never quite understood the reason which underlay the determination on no account to let him go home. He did not think of himself as a 'folk legend' but as a hard working member of the royal family. If at first some of his relations failed to see that Wallis was the perfect woman, he was convinced they would soon come to realize how perfect she was. He himself never had the slightest doubt as to her perfection.

Walter Monckton had taken on the same work for George VI as he had done for Edward VIII. Then and always he remained a good friend to the Duke of Windsor who was very fond of him, but he also sympathized with the new King and understood his hesitation to welcome home a brother who had formerly dominated him to such a marked degree. When from time to time Walter Monckton visited the Windsors after their marriage he sensed the frustration of the Duke, who had wrongly imagined he could go home once his brother was firmly established on the Throne.

Although, as we know, this was not to be, the Duke at that time was still hoping to be able to serve his country. One of the worst miseries of pre-war Britain (and it is by no means over, even now) was bad housing. The Duke of Windsor, as Prince and as King, had many times seen the degradation of it. In 1930 Queen Mary had written to him: 'I don't think there would be much discontent if only the people were housed properly.' Discontent is, rather naturally, dreaded by kings and queens; the Duke of Windsor saw the problem in terms of men and women, citizens of a country then considered the richest and most powerful in the world, 'owning' a quarter of the globe and with a vast reserve of unemployed labour, yet governed by politicians with neither ability nor imagination.

When, in 1937, the Duke was invited to go to Germany and see what had been done there about low-cost housing he accepted. It was exactly the sort of non-political, non-party problem where he thought he might be able to play some part before too long. The politicians did not see it in this light. Although incapable of devising a solution, they were determined to allow no-one else to help, whether it be Lloyd George with his dynamism, or the Duke of Windsor with his almost magic popularity. It was unrealistic to imagine they would react in any other way. We have seen that Lloyd George went so far as to attribute the 'alacrity to dethrone him' to the fact that he had 'as Prince and Sovereign exposed the continual neglect by Government of chronic distress, poverty and bad housing conditions amongst the people in his realm.'

While he was King he had been visited by his cousin, the Duke of Saxe-Coburg and Gotha, an enthusiastic National Socialist who had brought messages from Hitler. The Duke of Windsor's love of Germany was inborn. 'Every drop of blood in my veins is German,' he said* – a slight exaggeration. He was anything but a Nazi, for obvious reasons; he was a convinced monarchist and a firm believer in the multi-racial Empire to which he had devoted so much time and energy all his life.

Dr Ley, the Minister responsible for housing, showed the Windsors round. In her memoirs the Duchess says she disliked Ley, and no doubt he was a rough and ready sort of man. His position was Reich Organizations leader. The German Labour Front (DAF) had thirty million members, and it regularly received ninety-five per cent of the subscriptions due, a notable expression of the German workers' confidence in Ley and the DAF. With this vast wealth the DAF built housing for its members, as well as holiday cruise vessels, convalescent homes and so forth.

While they were in Berlin, the Windsors drove to Karinhall and lunched with General Goering. A few months previously Lord Londonderry, a former Secretary of State for Air, had invited Goering to stay at Londonderry House for the Coronation, but he had declined. He said that in his opinion Anglo-German relations had cooled since the year before, when Lord Londonderry had been to a shoot at Karinhall.

In Bavaria, after visiting the new housing estates, the Windsors went to the Berghof, where the Duke had a talk with Hitler while the Duchess chatted with the entourage in the famous room with its view of range upon range of mountains. Although the Duke spoke fluent German, Hitler used his interpreter, Paul Schmidt. From time to time the Duke was displeased with the translation of his words, saying sharply 'Falsch übersetzt!' and

*In conversation with the author.

144

*In Germany in 1937: the Duke and Duchess with Dr Ley (left), the Reich Organizations leader*

*Left: The Duke and Duchess being welcomed by Hitler on their visit to the Berghof*

*Above: The Duke and Duchess of Windsor leaving the Berghof*

making Herr Schmidt try again. The transcript of their conversation has vanished from the captured files.

What did Hitler and the Duke make of one another?* There were certain areas of agreement between them – admiration for the British Empire, hatred of communism. Hitler would undoubtedly have been sensible of the well-known charm of his guest, but as a realist he was aware that any usefulness to himself or to his policy with regard to Britain that might have resulted from the fact that the Duke was friendly disposed toward Germany, had been thrown away in 1936 when he abdicated. He would therefore not have given any more importance to the visit than he did to the visits of other prominent foreigners who came to see him. The previous year he had had a long talk with Lloyd George, for example, who subsequently wrote enthusiastically in the English press about what he had seen in Germany. But Lloyd George was out of office and destined to remain so.

In 1937 there was as yet no war fever in England; it only began to build up after the Munich settlement in the autumn of 1938. The Foreign Office was against this visit of the Duke to Germany and the British Ambassador did not call upon him, though the Chargé d'Affaires did. This reflected official disapproval of the Duke taking any initiative; English officialdom hoped that by ignoring him he would cease to exist. There was little point in the visit if under no circumstances was he to be allowed to return to England, but at that time he assumed that he would be home before too long. What Ley had done in Germany was what Lloyd George and others wished to do in Britain, and just as before the First World War it had been Germany to which Lloyd George looked as the first country to institute national insurance (detested by the Tories, (ninepence for fourpence,) so in 1937 it was the country which had solved the problem of unemployment, at the same time enriching itself with new roads, land reclamation and decent houses for its citizens.

The Windsors' visit to Germany was criticized at the time; Herbert Morrison in *Forward*, a Socialist weekly, asked why, if the Duke was so interested in housing, he did not study and read books on the subject. It was precisely because he had studied it that the Duke wished to see for himself what could be done in a practical way.

The plan was that the Duke and Duchess should next go to the United States for a similar tour. It had been their mysterious host

*The author, who saw Hitler from time to time, cannot remember hearing him mention the Duke or the Duchess of Windsor. More than once he said that England was fortunate to have '*diese kleine Prinzessin*'. He had seen Princess Elizabeth, then aged about ten, on cinema news-reels, and considered she was '*ein fabelhaftes Kind*', a marvellous child.

at Candé who had suggested they should go to Germany, but no practical help was needed from him because the Germans were pleased to show their successful projects to foreign notabilities. In America, however, Charles Bedaux himself arranged for the Duke to see low-cost housing and industrial installations. The Duchess in particular was delighted at the idea of going home to America; they were invited to the White House and the British Ambassador was to give a dinner party for them on their arrival in Washington.

They had no idea that, because of the way he had made his fortune, (a system he had devised for speeding up work in factories, rightly considered 'inhuman') Mr Bedaux was the *bête noire* of organized labour in the United States. They soon found out. The whole trip was cancelled, a great disappointment to the Duchess. Perhaps it was just as well, for the mere idea of the visit had caused concern in England. As the British Ambassador, Sir Ronald Lindsay, explained to Undersecretary of State Sumner Welles:

> The Ambassador . . . had found on the part of all the governing class in England a very vehement feeling of indignation against the course of the Duke of Windsor, based in part on the resentment created by his relinquishment of his responsibilities and in even greater part due to the apparent unfairness of his present attitude with regard to his brother, the King. The Ambassador said that in Court circles and in the Foreign Office and on the part of the heads of political parties, this feeling bordered on the stage of hysteria.

When the stage of hysteria is reached there is little to be done, reason flies out of the window. What is interesting looking back is that these brothers, the Duke of Windsor and King George VI, formerly devoted to one another, each felt that the other was being 'unfair'. Perhaps they were both right. The King had been landed with a task he did not want, and he felt the least the Duke could do would be to leave him alone to get on with it in his own way. The Duke, as he had written twenty years before to Lord Stamfordham, was only trained to do the job of a royal prince, which he must have known he did supremely well. That was the trouble.

It is a curious fact that it was the very people who had tended to be critical of Edward VIII as Prince of Wales and as King, the stuffiest part of the establishment, who were indignant because of his 'relinquishment of his responsibilities.' Since they now had an ideal King and Queen it is hard to understand their 'vehement feeling of indignation'. The Ambassador rightly stressed the fact that it was the 'governing class', and doubtless he might have added the Churches to his list.

# XV

# *War*

'Let there be light!' said God, and there was
light.
'Let there be blood,' says man, and there's a
sea.

*Byron*

The Windsors moved into La Croë, a large white house with green shutters near the sea at Cap d'Antibes, in the summer of 1938. They both liked the house, and it was there that real happiness began for them. As it was only partly furnished they brought many of their belongings from England, and with the Duke's treasures from the Fort round them they began to feel at home. The Duchess put her grandmother's rocking chair from Baltimore in her bedroom.

They needed more servants than at the Hôtel Meurice, who were engaged for them in England. The Duchess was superstitious, she loved lucky charms and dreaded evil omens. One very pretty girl who was taken on at that time had a strong impression that part of the reason she got the job was because of her fair colouring. The Duchess wanted only blond people round her; she thought they brought her luck. She was a good employer, generous and well-liked by her household, but she was a perfectionist. She kept a little book near her to make notes about any imperfections, and she used it freely. She had inherited from her mother a love of good food, and in France she had come to understand the importance of wine. She said she wanted the Duke to live like a king, and so he did. They both ate very little and when they were alone the food was plain, grilled lean meat, salad and fruit. They were keen weight-watchers.

The Duchess had unerring taste in clothes and in jewellery. The Duke loved giving her jewellery, and he became quite an expert. M. Jacques Cartier was once heard to say: 'Son Altesse Royale knows more about diamonds than I do!'. A hairdresser did her hair every day. This determination always to look her best, never to allow her very high standard to fall, continued for the rest of her

*Above: The Château de la Croë at Cap d'Antibes, which was leased by the Duke and Duchess in 1938*

*Overleaf: Cecil Beaton's photograph of Wallis, 1938*

151

life. (Forty years after this, at the age of eighty, she still had her fine skin; there were no wrinkles, no crows feet round her dark blue eyes, astonishing in someone so thin.) She took no exercise, she was a worrier, plagued by intermittent duodenal ulcers, and she slept badly, but she kept all this to herself. The Duke, on the other hand, slept well and played golf whenever he could, keeping himself fit. At La Croë the Duchess seemed to have regained all her old gaiety, living for the day. She had always been an avid reader of papers and magazines, now she read biographies and histories at night when she could not sleep.

They entertained friends at La Croë, giving dinner parties and going out to houses along the coast. One of their guests, Prince Jean-Louis de Lucinge, remembers seeing on the hall table the Duke's programme for the day. It was an invariable rule that he should have this, even in summer in the South of France. He liked to know who the guests, if any, were going to be, where they were dining, what time he was meeting someone for golf. None of it was important, but all his life he had been accustomed to a programme and the Duchess wisely saw to it that he should have one. She herself was never a moment late, being a very punctual person; his programme helped the Duke to be punctual too. They led the life that many rich people do, in his case from necessity, not choice. The only job he was trained for was closed to him.

That autumn the Windsors moved into a Paris house for the winter, in the Boulevard Suchet. Like La Croë, it was more luxurious than beautiful. It was big, with several drawing rooms ideal for parties, and it was near the Bois de Boulogne for walking their dogs and not far from the golf links at St Cloud. The Duchess took endless trouble with furnishing and decorating this house.

The Comtesse René de Chambrun remembers[*] dining at Boulevard Suchet soon after it was finished. She is the daughter of Pierre Laval, with whom the Duke, as Prince of Wales, had had a long talk at the British Embassy a few years previously, when Laval had stressed the importance for France and England to remain on good terms with Italy rather than driving it into alliance with Germany.

Josée de Chambrun says that as she and her husband walked up the stairs the footmen in their scarlet livery made an impression of rare elegance. On the dining-room table, lit by many candles, were gold goblets filled with lilies. She says of the Duchess: '*Elle donnait toujours à ses maisons un air de fête.*' Nobody is more competent than Mme de Chambrun to judge two things to which the French attach great importance in a woman – her clothes and her table – because she herself has great chic and provides delicious food. A

---

[*]In conversation with the author.

friend of the Windsors for almost forty years, she awards the Duchess top marks for both.

Before the war, as Mme de Chambrun says, the Duchess was *'très Mainbocher'*. We have seen that he made her wedding gown and her trousseau. In this connection Jane Lady Abdy describes* a fashion show in 1979 of old dresses, 1900 to 1945; 'among the Doucets and Redferns was a marvellous dress made for Mrs Simpson by Mainbocher in 1935. When I saw it I really understood her legendary chic, it was so supremely elegant one longed to wear it and to be thin enough to do so.' Mainbocher's clothes were notable for their extreme simplicity, they relied upon perfect cut, and ideally were worn by small, slender women. The Duchess was therefore his perfect client.

Among the many visitors to the Windsors at the Boulevard Suchet were the Lindberghs. Mrs Lindbergh and the Duchess agreed how tiresome it was for their husbands never to be able to go anywhere without being recognized. Charles Lindbergh saw eye to eye with the Duke in thinking war with Germany would be a tragedy.

The international situation was grave. The Duke was strongly in favour of peace; he was one of those far-sighted enough to realize that a war with Germany, win or lose, would be disastrous for Britain. He thought it would probably be the end of the British Empire. That many, perhaps most people would now find this desirable is neither here nor there. In his opinion it would be a tragedy. There was nothing pro-German about his point of view, it was pro-British. As an ex-serviceman who had seen the horrors and disasters of war he could not bear to contemplate a new generation wiped out as his own generation had been. In England, however, most of his political friends took the opposite point of view and were against the Munich settlement: Winston Churchill, Anthony Eden and Duff Cooper among them.

The following summer the Windsors went back to La Croë and they were there when war was declared. At the end of August the Duke sent a telegram to Hitler in which 'as a citizen of the world' he begged him not to plunge the world into war. Hitler replied that he had never wanted war with England and that if it took place it would not be his fault. On 3 September, on his way to swim, the Duke was called to the telephone and the British Ambassador in Paris gave him the news. The Duchess says his comment was: 'Great Britain has just declared war on Germany, and I am afraid in the end this may open the way for world communism.'

He telephoned Walter Monckton in London, saying: 'I want to

*In a letter to the author.

offer my services in any capacity my brother deems appropriate and I must return to Britain.' The censor insisted that all telephone calls abroad must be made in French which was difficult for the Duke and for Walter Monckton, neither of whom could speak the language easily. Three days later Monckton arrived at La Croë, sitting beside the pilot in a small Leopard Moth, to discuss plans. Mr Chamberlain offered the Duke a choice of two jobs, either Deputy Regional Commissioner in Wales, or liaison officer with the British Military Mission to General Gamelin. The Duke preferred to serve in England, but ever since his marriage he had blamed himself for not making certain at the time of his Abdication that the Duchess should be properly treated; rather naturally he had no more guessed than had anyone else what was in store. Nothing that had happened since gave him much confidence in the good faith of the authorities, but he thought something as tremendous as war might be the catalyst which could smooth out the family difficulties.

After frantic packing the Windsors motored to Cherbourg, stopping in Paris on the way for the Duke to see the British Ambassador. They offered La Croë to be a hospital for the wounded, and they had bidden most of their household farewell some days before, those who were English having gone home to do war work. At Cherbourg a destroyer commanded by Lord Louis Mountbatten awaited them. This had been arranged by Winston Churchill, now First Lord of the Admiralty, and he had sent his son Randolph, wearing the uniform of the 4th Hussars, to greet them on his behalf. The Duke noticed that Randolph's spurs were strapped on upside down. When they arrived at Portsmouth there was a guard of honour for the Duke, and the Commander in Chief, Admiral Sir William James, invited the Windsors to stay the night. Next day, since the Duke was offered nowhere to stay, they went to the Metcalfes' house in Sussex.

The Duke was up and down to London and whenever he was glimpsed by members of the public he was enthusiastically welcomed. This was noticed and it was not liked.

One day the Duke and Duchess lunched with Lady Colefax, Harold Nicolson and H.G. Wells were there. Nicolson says the Duke in his uniform looked very young and very pleased to be home in England. As they left the house, Nicolson said to Wells: 'Admit that man has charm.' 'Glamour,' said H. G. Wells.

The Duke saw the King and discussed with him which job he should take, and the King seemed to agree that he should be Deputy Regional Commissioner. But a few days later the CIGS informed him that he was assigned to the British Military Mission

155

*The Duke and Duchess on HMS* Kelly, *nine days after the outbreak of war. On the left is Randolph Churchill, sent by Winston Churchill, first Lord of the Admiralty, in September 1939 to greet the Duke and Duchess on his behalf; behind the Duke stands his cousin, Lord Louis Mountbatten, who was in command of the* Kelly, *and in the background is Major Metcalfe*

at Vincennes and was to report for duty forthwith. The Duchess says in her memoirs: 'The civil defence job was never mentioned again. David and I suspected – perhaps unfairly – that some of the older members of the Court had recommended that, rather than encourage any possible revival of the former King's popularity, he be posted ... outside the country.' They sailed from Portsmouth to Cherbourg in a destroyer on a rough day late in September, with Major Metcalfe as the Duke's A.D.C. The authorities in England breathed again.

Because the Duke's job with Major-General Sir Richard Howard-Vyse at Vincennes entailed a good deal of travelling the Windsors did not open the house in Boulevard Suchet. Instead they stayed at the Trianon Palace Hotel in Versailles, where the Duchess busied herself making parcels of comforts for the troops. The organization was called *Les Colis du Trianon* and had been started by Lady Mendl who lived near the Petit Trianon.

Before the war she and Sir Charles Mendl had given enjoyable parties at their Versailles house. He was press attaché at the Embassy and Lady Mendl was an American interior decorator of wide renown. She was quite old but she stood on her head for a long time each morning, a habit to which she attributed her health and vitality. She was luxury-loving, and Mrs Rex Benson* thinks perhaps she gave the Duchess a few tips about how the rich live, such as taking their own fine sheets if they stayed at an hotel, but as the Duchess took to luxury with the greatest of ease Lady Mendl's advice may not have been necessary. As a rule she did help Americans visiting Paris, by making suggestions as to how they might spend more money. Now, however, there was war, and Lady Mendl's energy was diverted to *Les Colis du Trianon*.

Prince Jean-Louis de Lucinge remembers having dinner at the Mendls' during this period of the phoney war. The Duke was away with the army. The Duchess was playing backgammon with Noël Coward when the butler approached and said quietly: 'Your Grace, His Royal Highness on the telephone.' The Duchess, absorbed in her game, did not hear. The butler spoke a little louder. 'Your Royal Highness, His Royal Highness on the telephone.' As she still paid no attention the butler almost shouted: 'Excuse me Your Majesty, His Royal Highness on the telephone.' The Duchess got up to follow him, saying to her companions as she did so: 'He's never heard what happened.'

Soon after this the Duchess went back to Boulevard Suchet and opened part of the house; the Duke was there from time to time. Mrs Rex Benson called on them one evening and found him

*In conversation with the author.

157

*The Duke arriving at the War Office in Whitehall*

*Above: The Duchess of Windsor as an officer in the French Women's Ambulance Corps*

*Below: The Duke of Windsor on one of his tours of inspection of the front line in France, November 1939*

knitting a muffler for *Les Colis du Trianon*. The Duchess now joined the French Red Cross and was kept very busy making frequent visits to hospitals near the Maginot Line, delivering bandages and plasma. There were plenty of hospitals but there were no wounded because there was no fighting. Everyone had imagined it was going to be like the First War over again.

Major Metcalfe was with the Duke as ADC, and he stayed at the Ritz. He often wrote to his wife, letters just like the ones from Enzesfeld three years before; sometimes full of complaints and sometimes saying what a delightful companion the Duke had been. These letters are fairly harmless in themselves and are probably typical of the attitude of nearly every employee dependant upon the moods of his employer. Whether their author would have wished them to be published in the lifetime of the Duchess is another matter. Major Gray Phillips, a man of great charm, joined their staff at Boulevard Suchet as comptroller; he helped the Windsors in every possible way, and stayed with them wherever they might be for many years.

After one of his tours of inspection of the front line the Duke sent a despatch to Major General Howard-Vyse, who wrote to the War Office: 'The Duke of Windsor has produced a valuable report on the defence.' He saw clearly that preparations for defence were inadequate, anti-tank crews insufficiently trained and so forth. One of Metcalfe's complaints was that although he accompanied the Duke on his tour the despatch was not shown to him.

On 10 May the Germans began their advance in the West, by-passing the Maginot Line and overrunning the inadequate defences observed by the Duke. On the 16th the Duke took the Duchess to Biarritz, returning at once to the Military Mission in Paris. A fortnight later, with the Germans near Paris and the *débâcle* obvious to all, he left Biarritz and took the Duchess to La Croë. Major Metcalfe went back to England.

A few days later Major Gray Phillips joined them at La Croë. It had taken him four days of hitch-hiking, the roads choked with refugees, his uniform was crumpled and covered in dust. The whole of France seemed to be on the move, cars abandoned for lack of petrol were strewn beside the roads leading south and west; families, with their belongings piled on handcarts, or carrying as much as they could, were obeying the instinct that makes a civilian population flee from advancing armies. Like everyone else the Windsors got their only news from the wireless. When Italy entered the war they were advised by Major Dodds, the British Consul at Nice, to leave for Spain. Dodds had received instructions to burn his papers and he had a *laisser passer* from the Spanish

Consul. They travelled west. When they came to barricades designed to hold up the Italian advance, manned by veterans of the First War who were indisposed to let them through, the Duke got out of his car and spoke to them: '*Je suis le Prince de Galles. Laissez-moi passer s'il vous plaît.*' He was always recognized and it worked every time. On such occasions 'magnetic charm' is a powerful asset. They had no proper papers and were held up at the frontier for some hours, but finally the whole party crossed into Spain.

In Madrid the British Ambassador was the Duke's old friend Sir Samuel Hoare, who told them that the Prime Minister, Winston Churchill, was sending flying boats to Lisbon to bring them home, and that the Duke of Westminster had offered them Eaton Hall in Cheshire. The Duke said he would go to England as soon as the question of the position of the Duchess was cleared up. On their previous visit to England a few months before she had been completely ignored and the Duke was not prepared to see this happen again. He has been criticized for making conditions about such a trifling matter when Britain was fighting for its life. In June 1940 there was, in fact, no fighting anywhere since France had signed an armistice. England was preparing to fight, but there was total calm until the following August and the outbreak of the Battle of Britain. If the Duke's request was so trifling why was it not complied with? It did not appear trifling to the authorities in Britain, and even Winston Churchill, who was so fond of the Duke and so well disposed, was unable to make them budge. He offered the Duke the governorship of the Bahamas, and it was accepted. Churchill's telegram ended with the significant words: 'I have done my best.'

On their arrival in Portugal the Windsors were met by the British Minister, Sir Walford Selby, whom they had known when he was *en poste* in Vienna. He installed them in a house by the sea at Cascais, belonging to the banker, Senhor Espirito Santo. While the Windsors' destination was still in doubt the Duke was visited by Miguel Primo de Rivera, brother of the celebrated José Antonio who had been murdered during the Spanish Civil War, and son of the old dictator. Rivera wanted to persuade the Duke to return to Spain rather than go to the Bahamas. He reported that he told the Duke that he might yet be called upon to play an important role and possibly ascend the English throne. The Duke was astonished and replied that under the British Constitution this would never be possible after the Abdication. The story goes that the Spaniards (and behind them, naturally, the Germans) wanted the Duke to stay so that he could be kidnapped at an appropriate moment and induced to work for Germany.

In the summer of 1940 there was a possibility that Britain might be defeated, and when a country is defeated in war, sooner or later the conqueror tries to find men among its citizens who would be prepared to take over the responsibility for running its affairs and negotiating the best terms possible with its conqueror. In Germany five years later, for example, Konrad Adenauer and Willy Brandt were willing to play such a part. It is most unlikely that Hitler himself would ever have imagined the patriot he knew the Duke to be could have been induced to do any such thing. Remembering his own feelings at the end of the First World War, he must have known it would be unthinkable. Also, quite apart from patriotic sentiment, for the Duke, having abdicated, to 'ascend the English throne' would have been highly dishonourable.

At the same time, since it is the duty of officials to prepare for any contingency, it is not impossible that the Germans on the spot and their Spanish friends thought the Duke might have his uses, and that they therefore hoped he would stay in Europe. It would have been utterly out of character for him to allow himself to be thus used, and among his own countrymen even those who, for one reason or another, disliked him have never believed in its possibility. There is a world of difference between a passionate desire for peace and a readiness to work for a victorious foreign power.

During the First World War the enemy was a Germany where the Duke had spent happy months as a boy, and almost every sector of the German army was led by near relations of his. The British royal family did not greet the outbreak of war in 1914 with the insouciant excitement that a large number of the less thoughtful of their subjects displayed. Yet, as we have seen, the Prince's only wish had been to get into active service. In the Second War he would have preferred a negotiated peace to the destruction of Europe and the loss of the Empire, but this he must have known was out of the question since the fall of France.

Another clumsy effort to induce the Duke to stay was made when he was told that the British Secret Service planned to get him to the Bahamas and then murder him. Walter Monckton flew to Lisbon and had a long talk with the Duke. An extra detective was provided, and after a tiresome wait for a ship to take them across the Atlantic the Duke and Duchess left for Bermuda and thence for the Bahamas. They wanted to go to America on the way, but President Roosevelt declined. In November he had an election coming up and was going to win by promising to keep the United States neutral. The isolationists would have made great propaganda if he had received such a prominent Englishman.

# XVI

# *The Bahamas*

What is hard today is to censor one's own
thoughts;
To sit by and see the blind man on the
sightless horse, riding into the abyss.

*Arthur Waley*

The Bahamas are a group of islands which geographically form a continuation of the Florida cays. Government House stands on a hill and from its pillared façade there is a view over the sea, while from the back it looks over gardens to the town of Nassau. Providence Island, though not the biggest, is the most heavily populated of the islands in the Bahamas.

The very hottest time of the year in the Bahamas is mid-August, and that is when the Windsors arrived. The Duchess says that during the reception of the Duke as Governor both he and the Chief Justice were pouring with sweat and their signatures were just two blots on the page. Eighteenth-century Nassau is very pretty with its immensely tall palm trees and Georgian architecture, and Government House is just like the 'colonial style' houses in the American South that the Duchess remembered from her child-hood. When she saw it she declared it absolutely lovely.

But the old house was shabby and needed renovating, and the Windsors telegraphed Mr and Mrs Frederick Sigrist to ask whether they could rent their house while the work was done. The reply was no, not rent, but that the Sigrists would lend it with pleasure. It is a delightful, comfortable house built on coral foundations above the sea on Prospect Ridge, with a large garden. The Windsors gratefully settled in. Frederick Sigrist was a brilliant aeronautical engineer, the creator, with Sir Thomas Sopwith, of the Hawker-Siddely Aircraft Company; he was about to leave for California where he advised the Americans on the manufacture of Hurricane Fighters.

Hot for about three months, the rest of the year the Bahamas bask in perpetual summer. Like all places with a really lovely climate, in those days there were plenty of insects to annoy; they annoyed the Duchess, who complained loudly of being eaten alive.

*Above: Government House, Nassau*

*Below: The Duke of Windsor taking his oath of office as Governor of the Bahamas*

There are beautiful gardens, and the sea is exactly the perfect temperature to swim in. Miami is about half an hour away by air. The Duchess has always been the subject of silly stories, and it was widely believed that she went to get her hair done in Miami once a week. In fact, as is well known, she disliked flying, and there were plenty of hairdressers in Nassau, but she did sometimes make shopping expeditions to Miami to buy garden furniture.

The Duchess says the Duke fitted into his role as Governor with the greatest of ease. She was busy as head of the Red Cross and of the Daughters of the British Empire. As always, she excelled as a hostess. In the newly done-up Government House she gave dinner parties for the local politicians, smoothing many difficulties. The Duke bought a cabin cruiser he called the *Gemini* (the sign of the Zodiac under which the Duchess was born) so that they could visit the out-islands, of which there are about seven hundred. Governorship of the Bahamas was very far from being the war service he would have chosen, but the Duke determined to do the job well.

The Duke of Windsor was very partial to millionaires who had made their money themselves. Any fool can inherit money, it was self-made men who had glamour for him. He felt about them as an ordinary snob might feel about people of ancient lineage going back into the mists of time. In the Bahamas there were several of these, to the Duke, fascinating men. Among them was Sir Harry Oakes, an American who had struck gold in Canada and taken Canadian citizenship, and Sir Harold Christie, a property tycoon who made a fortune by being one of the first to realize the wonderful possibilities of the Bahamas as a winter playground for the rich and in particular for Americans. The islands are only a few minutes by air from Miami, they are uncrowded, some of them empty, with beaches of silvery sand and seas of palest most brilliant blue.

After Pearl Harbor, war approached the Bahamas. Tourists no longer came from America, and in their place there were survivors from ships torpedoed by U-boats. The Red Cross ladies worked overtime.

In 1942 the Colonial office in London conceived the idea that a U-boat might kidnap the Windsors and hold them as hostages, therefore a company of Cameron Highlanders was sent to the island. The troops put barbed wire round Government House, then they practised mock raids. They had an amusing time creeping through the barbed wire at night and taking Major Gray Phillips prisoner while he slept. Soon afterwards the Cameron Highlanders were needed for more serious work.

The Americans built an airfield called Windsor Field, to be shared by them and the RAF. The local black labourers considered

*Left: The Duchess, as President of the Bahamas Red Cross Association, showing the Duke some of the supplies to be sent to England*

*Below: The Duke and Duchess visiting two survivors of a sea rescue, December 1940*

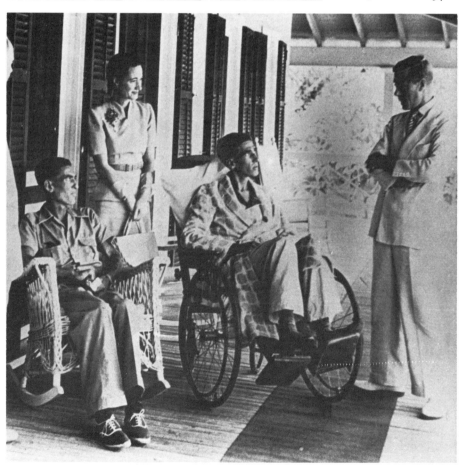

their wages were low compared with what the Americans earned. In May the Windsors were in Washington staying at the British Embassy with Lord and Lady Halifax when a message came from Nassau that serious rioting had broken out. The mob had smashed all the windows and looted the shops in Bay Street and drunk all the liquor they could find. The Duke flew straight back. The riot act was read, martial law was declared and the Cameron Highlanders with the police had no trouble in restoring order.

Wages were raised by the Americans to a more equitable level. The Duke encouraged agriculture as far as possible, but the riches of the Bahamas came from the tourists and only after the war did the islands boom again. The most difficult years were those when the Duke of Windsor was Governor.

The Windsors went fairly often to Washington, and lunching one day at the White House with President Roosevelt, they found their old friends Herman and Katherine Rogers were fellow guests. When the Duchess invited them to stay in Nassau, Katherine Rogers said they could not accept as they had no passports. Mr Roosevelt immediately got in touch with the passport office so that they were able to go, a great pleasure for the Duchess.

On another occasion, when Churchill was in America to address Congress the Duke and Duchess went to listen to the speech, and were given an ovation: 'As the Duke descended to his seat in the front row, he got as much clapping as Winston, or more, by which we were surprised', wrote Lord Moran. The Windsors also visited a ranch belonging to the Duke in Canada, and they went to Baltimore where they stayed with the Duchess's uncle, General Henry Warfield. There were always crowds to greet them; ten thousand people, headed by Aunt Bessie, were at the railway station in Washington when they arrived the first time.

In July 1943 Sir Harry Oakes was brutally murdered in his bed. Sir Harold Christie was staying with him at Westbourne at the time.* The Duke called in the Miami police; he was criticized for not immediately getting in touch with Scotland Yard, but in his opinion and that of his officials speed was more important than protocol; Miami was on his doorstep, London thousands of miles away. According to a doctor who examined the body these detectives from Miami were so ill-equipped that muddle was certain. He formed the opinion that Oakes had been hit with a poker while asleep and that he never recovered consciousness or moved again, though he was then hit three more blows, yet the detectives pro-

*One evening, years later, the author was dining with Lord Beaverbrook at his villa on Cap d'Ail when Sir Harold Christie was a guest. Beaverbrook's opening gambit was, 'Come on, Harold, tell us how you murdered Harry Oakes', a joke which evoked a tired smile from Christie.

ceeded on the assumption that there had been 'a running fight'. Some people thought it was a mafia murder but the mystery was never solved. It caused shock waves all through the colony, and the Duke was genuinely sorry, for he had become fond of Harry Oakes who was the sort of rough diamond that he appreciated.

The Duchess created a maternity care centre for the blacks in Nassau, the first of its kind in the Bahamas, she devoted a lot of time to it as she also did to her canteen. A young RAF officer who was often invited to Government House says how popular the Duchess was with British and Commonwealth servicemen of all ranks. She worked really hard in the canteen and they got to know her at first hand. He mentions her 'true kind-heartedness'. This is interesting, because one of the reasons why the authorities in England wanted the Duke to serve overseas rather than at home subsequently turned out to be that they thought if he visited the troops with the Duchess, there might be demonstrations against her. In fact, people in the know feared the very opposite. The Duke's popularity was bad enough; what if the Duchess, with her breezy, friendly manner, went down all too well?

When they left the Bahamas in 1945 gifts were showered upon the Windsors, and they were touched by evidence of the affectionate regard they were held in by all sections of the community. They stayed for a few months in America and returned to France in the autumn.

# XVII

# The Windsors
# in France

I have good experience of this world, and I
know what it is to be a subject and what to
be a sovereign. Good neighbours I have had,
and I have met with bad.

*Queen Elizabeth I*

Despite six years of war, and the occupation of Paris, the house in Boulevard Suchet and its contents had remained intact, and it soon wore its old aspect once again. But the Windsors had only rented it and they now had to move. They first lived in the Rue de la Faisanderie, but after a while they acquired a house in a big garden in the Bois de Boulogne belonging to the French Government. They paid a nominal rent, and there they stayed for the rest of their lives. General de Gaulle had used it just after the war; Gaston Palewski, the Gaullist Minister who was a friend of the General and also of the Windsors, describes the tremendous contrast of dining there first with one and then with the others. The silences, the whispered conversations, the ascetic way of life of de Gaulle were very unlike the rich and beautiful table of the Duchess, with its talk that was always amusing and sometimes brilliant, fantastic food and sumptuous wines.

When the ship bringing the Windsors back to Europe had called at an English port, journalists asked the Duke whether he would like to live in England, and he said yes, he would. A whole decade and the war had passed since the Abdication, yet nothing had changed. 'They' were still concerned to keep him out of the country if possible.

Truth to tell, it was quite easy now. There is no question but that the Duchess preferred France. Contrary to what is often said, they had dozens of French friends, and the things she excelled at, her clothes, her food, were French. Her ideal was to live in France and visit America from time to time, and this became the pattern of their life. They usually stayed in France from April until after Christmas, then they went to America, to the Waldorf Tower in New York where they rented a lovely flat with a spectacular view, and to Palm Beach to stay with friends. There was a persistent

*Left: The Duke with his mother, Queen Mary, in the gardens of Marlborough House in 1945*

*Above: The Duchess at the Paris Horse Show in 1949*

rumour that when they were at Palm Beach they made boring people pay them large sums for the privilege of having the Windsors to dine. It would have been an excellent idea, but unfortunately it never in fact happened.

The Duke was now over fifty, and although he would have liked to work (and it was a stupid waste to prevent it) he was perfectly happy not to. He offered his services as roving ambassador in the United States; he would have done a wonderful job, but needless to say the offer was turned down.

It is useless to pretend, as some of his biographers do, that the Duke was a sad exile. To reinforce this description they publish photographs showing him in the most unbecoming light. He did not much care for being photographed and all his life there had been a sad expression on his face except when he was actually smiling. Sometimes, caught unawares, he looked both sad and startled; then the photograph went on the front pages. For the funerals of Queen Mary and of King George VI he went to London, and rather naturally looked quite unhappy.

Only one thing made him miserable and that was if for some reason he was separated from the Duchess. In 1948 Winston Churchill sat next to Mabell, Lady Airlie one day at luncheon. She wrote: 'We talked of the Duke and Duchess of Windsor. Winston told me he himself had always liked her. "The Duke's love for her is one of the great loves of history," he said. "I saw him when she had gone away for a fortnight. He was miserable, haggard, dejected, not knowing what to do. Then I saw him when she had been back a day or two, he was a different man – gay, debonair, self-confident. Make no mistake, he can't live without her." '

The many people who saw him during these post-war years, particularly those who knew him well, never found him in the least sad. He may not (as the Duchess obviously did) have preferred Paris to London, but it made very little difference because the two cities are now so close that all his old friends came frequently, some of them almost too frequently. As to the Windsors' American friends, they saw them in New York and at Palm Beach and they came over to Paris in droves at certain seasons of the year. The problem was not too few friends but too many.

They considered buying La Croë, which was now for sale. They went back there and found that the Italian soldiers had looted very little, but the South of France had changed and did not attract them as formerly. It had the disadvantage of being far from Paris, too far to go for a day or two, as the Duchess refused to fly.

Like Sydney Smith, she had no relish for the country, 'a kind

*The Duke with Sir Winston and Lady Churchill at Antibes after the war*

*The Duke and Duchess at Portofino, one of their favourite holiday resorts*

of healthy grave', as he called it. But the Windsors still thought of getting a house in the sun. There was an idea they might build at Marbella in Spain, and the Duchess wanted her old friend from Peking days, Georges Sebastian, now famous for his skill and taste, to design a villa. It came to nothing; they needed to be near Paris and to have three houses was beyond their means. There is pretty country within reach of Paris, and that she could relish up to a point, while the Duke could make a garden.

In the early fifties she found an old mill, the Moulin de la Tuilerie, in the Vallée de Chevreuse, twenty-five miles from Paris. (It is near the village of Gif-sur-Yvette, then a pretty little place, now unimaginably hideous with blocks of appalling flats.) It belonged to the painter Drian, and he was willing to sell. A small seventeenth-century house on a rushing mill stream, it had a cobbled courtyard and there were out-houses and a large barn. All this the Duchess transformed into bedrooms and bathrooms and drawing rooms and dining rooms, some big and some minute. Like many royal personages the Duke loved small, cosy, snug rooms. (This has always been so, as witness the *petits apartements* in the Château de Versailles.) If there was a big luncheon party two round tables were put in the former barn, now a large and cheerful room, one presided over by her and the other by him. Dinner was usually in the dining room of the main house, and the Duke wore his kilt in the evening. If they were alone or with one or two guests they lunched in an outdoor loggia facing the garden in summer.

Helped by Mr Russell Page the Duke made an English garden, with two herbaceous borders and a lawn between leading down to the Mérantaise, a swiftly running stream. There was a small steep hill beyond with trees, and the Duke piped water to the top so that it splashed down among the rocks and alpine plants. He called it Cardiac Hill because people with weak hearts refused to climb up it for a view of the garden. There was a walled kitchen garden and glass houses for flowers in winter; the Duchess's rooms were always full of flowers. The head gardener was Alsatian; the Duke was not fluent in French and he could talk to this gardener in German.

Both of the Windsors loved the Mill, the first house that had belonged to them in all their married life. She enjoyed choosing furniture and colours and stuffs for the rooms and he enjoyed making his garden. It only took forty minutes to drive down from their Paris house and he went there often in the afternoon to work in the garden. At week-ends they had friends staying and people came in for luncheon or dinner. It was the prettiest, most cheerful place

*Above: The Moulin de la Tuilerie in the Vallée de Chevreuse, with part of the Duke's garden in the foreground*

*Right: The Duke and Duchess at the Mill. The Duke wore his Stuart tartan kilt in the evening*

*Sidney, the footman, with some of the pugs, at the Windsors' Paris house*

imaginable, with crackling wood fires in winter and in summer the bright flowers.

Guests invited to dine at the Mill in winter drove down a short drive to gates, where the gate-keeper peered through the dark at the car to be sure it was in order for it to enter the precincts, then across a cobbled yard to the house. The front door opened at once, a footman was posted there to keep a look out so that not a second was lost. The front door led straight into the hall, where the Duke and Duchess with the other guests were gathered round a fire with huge glowing logs burning on the wide hearth. The men were in dinner jackets, the women in evening dress, but the Duke wore his Stuart tartan kilt. The Windsors both had the gift of making their guests feel as welcome as if their arrival had been long looked forward to. A variety of cocktails and whisky were offered round and hot savouries in silver dishes, everyone standing or sitting near the fire. After about twenty minutes, soon after nine, dinner was announced to the Duchess and she led the women into the dining room next door, then the Duke made the men go in before him. The table was very pretty and gay with many candles and flowers (the really beautiful things were in Paris; at the Mill countrified simplicity was the note).

If there were eight people or less, the conversation was general. There was an atmosphere of great gaiety and amusement, while all the topics of the day were discussed. The Duke loved talking politics and both he and the Duchess, as devoted readers of newspapers and magazines, were well-informed about French, English and American affairs. There was a certain amount of gossip about mutual friends, and here the Duchess succeeded in being amusing without being spiteful, which is not always as easy as it sounds.

A typical dinner might be *filets* of *barbue* in a rich sauce, plain roast partridges with salad, an iced pudding and a savoury. The Duke liked the old English custom of a savoury at the end of dinner with which to drink port. It is unknown in France; the French say 'it is impossible to eat scrambled eggs after chocolate ice.' But the Duchess's savouries half conquered her French guests; nobody refused them. The wines were well chosen to go with the food, a Rhine wine with the fish, an old claret with the game and a sauterne with the pudding. Another English custom always observed by the Windsors was that when the women left the dining room the Duke stayed behind with the other men.

The Duchess led the way up a tiny staircase, along a passage past her bedroom, and there, unexpectedly, was an enormous drawing room, formerly a loft. It had French windows leading to the garden; so hilly was the terrain that the Mill had these two levels, part of its charm. In winter the curtains were drawn, and a fire with giant logs would be burning. The predominant colours in this cheerful room were pink and apricot, the bright soft light was becoming, so that women were happy to feel they were looking their best.

After about half an hour the Duke reappeared, a large cigar in his hand, with his men guests. So also did footmen, offering champagne and whisky. There was more talk and more jokes, and at about half past twelve it was time to go. The Duchess said goodbye, the Duke insisted on accompanying the guests downstairs. The butler appeared with coats and the door was opened to let in a blast of freezing air. Implored by the guests to go back upstairs where it was warm, the Duke in his kilt, with bare knees, insisted on standing outside until the car moved off.

The Duchess now made a real effort to learn French. She asked Walter Lees, an English friend living in Paris, to find her a teacher. 'I would prefer a woman. I feel I can't go on making such foolish mistakes,' she wrote to him. The Duke contented himself with German and Spanish; he was pleased when visitors from Spain or from South America enabled him to air his Spanish.

James Pope-Hennessy says in his biography of Queen Mary that although she spent her life collecting she never bought a good picture. The same could be said of her daughter-in-law. The Paris house in particular became more and more royal, with incredible numbers of ornaments and knick-knacks. There was a whole table covered with Meissen pugs of all sizes.

The cairn terriers had long since been replaced by pugs, which snuffled and leaned heavily against the legs of the guests as pugs will. They were not allowed to get fat and the Duchess rationed them, so they were overjoyed when the black footman, Sidney, appeared to take them off for their dinner. They were loved and cherished by the Duke as well as the Duchess, but he dreaded her finding out about a pug show for fear she might buy several more.

In August the Windsors usually went to an hotel at Biarritz with the Dudleys. Grace Lady Dudley says she was 'very fond' of the Duchess, so 'quick, intuitive and generous',* and that the Duke and Lord Dudley had a wonderful time remembering the past. They played golf and went swimming: there were plenty of friends in the neighbourhood.

Sometimes they went to Venice where they also found many friends. During those years Carlos de Beistegui spent the summers at his Palazzo Labia, a gloriously beautiful palace. The big high room with Tiepolo frescoes of Antony and Cleopatra is perhaps

*In conversation with the author.

the loveliest in all Venice; Charlie Beistegui hung eight Venetian glass chandeliers, four high up and four lower, and kept the room practically empty – there were many other drawing-rooms where guests could sit. One day he asked the Duchess whether there was anything in particular she would care to see in Venice, because if so he would fetch her in his gondola. The answer was unexpected. 'Oh yes, I should love to see Countess – 's house,' she replied. Charlie Beistegui told the author: 'Of course we all love – but her house is *hideous*. However, the Duchess didn't think so, she told me after we had tea there it was her dream house.' The truth is that she preferred something up-to-date, bright and smart to real beauty.

Nevertheless in her own houses there were many beautiful objects and the dining-room table was always perfectly lovely, and always different, with silver, vermeil, porcelain.

The Duke still enjoyed his game of golf as much as ever. From Paris he played at St Cloud or St Germain, and as he preferred to eat no lunch the ideal time from his point of view was between 12.30 and 2 p.m., the sacred hour of *déjeuner* for the French, when there were few people about. His friends fell in with this plan. One was Sir Berkeley Ormerod, a former British Army golf champion. His wife Bea was the widow of Frederick Sigrist – it was she who had lent the Windsors her house near Nassau while Government House was done up. Bill Ormerod had been Director of Public Relations for the British Information Service in New York during the war, and the Duke made use of the BIS when researching for his autobiography, *A King's Story*. Bill cheerfully gave up his luncheon for the Duke's sake, who, when the game was finished, would ask for hot water to make tea with China tea leaves he brought in a little canister; he drank his tea while the starving Bill Ormerod ate a bun. (Incidentally, he says the Duke always insisted on paying his green fees, he mentions this because of stories about the Duke being stingy in small ways.)[*]

Sir Berkeley was an expert on Wall Street and had written a book on Dow Jones. This expertise fascinated the Duke, who found the book very interesting. The Windsors were rich, but extravagant in their mode of life, and with inflation creeping up the Duke tried to get the best advice on his investments.

In 1951 he sold his memoirs for enormous sums, about half a million pounds (when the pound was worth many times what it is now). The Duchess also made money with her memoirs, *The Heart has its Reasons*. The idea of actually earning money appealed greatly to the Duke, and when Jack Le Vien came to him with a

[*]In a letter to the author.

proposal that he should make a documentary film out of *A King's Story*, giving the Duke the same contract as had been agreed with Sir Winston Churchill's tough American lawyers a few years before, the Duke studied the contract for a very long time. Finally Jack Le Vien said: Sir, is there anything wrong with the contract? It is identical with the one we made with Sir Winston when we did a documentary film about him.' The Duke replied: 'I was just looking to see if there was anything about an expense account.'

These two books, *A King's Story* and *The Heart has its Reasons*, tell us a good deal about their authors and events in their lives. The Duke's is the better of the two and, although he was helped by a ghost-writer, his own voice can be heard. The Duchess on the other hand is more or less unrecognizable in her book. She was much more amusing and much more of a character than anyone could guess from reading it. The woman in *The Heart has its Reasons* could never have captivated for a lifetime the love and admiration of such a man as the Duke, formerly rather fickle and capricious. Both of the Windsors were perfectly capable of writing their autobiographies without help, and maybe it is a pity they did not do so.

James Pope-Hennessy often went to the Mill when he was writing his biography of Queen Mary to talk with the Duke. Later on, casting about for another subject, he thought he would like to do a book about the Windsors. When he spoke of it to the Duke, the response was surprising. 'What percentage of the money earned by your book on Queen Mary did the royal family get?' asked the Duke. 'Oh, they got nothing at all,' said James Pope-Hennessy. The Duke made it plain that if he were to co-operate with James he would expect to be paid. The huge sums he had made with his memoirs and the money he got from Jack Le Vien's film had sharpened his appetite. He could not see the point of giving his time to help with a biography which he was not at all sure he would approve of and over which he would exercise no control, and do it for nothing. He had a very practical view of money; it was almost as if he could see into the future, the inflation that was coming.

The Duke's love and need for the Duchess grew with the years and without doubt it imposed a strain. Sometimes she must have slightly regretted the old free days when she did what she liked and said whatever came into her head, before she became Duchess of Windsor. As Duff Cooper once said to her: 'You have all the disadvantages of royalty and none of its advantages.' Just occasionally she chose freedom.

It was in 1950 that the Windsors first made friends with Jimmy Donahue, a rich American whose mother was a Woolworth; he

*Above: The Duke and Duchess in 1951, celebrating the publication of his memoirs,* A King's Story

*Below: Jack Le Vien sitting with the Duke and Duchess in the gardens of the Mill, during the production of the film,* A King's Story, *1964*

*The Duke and Duchess dancing in the Hotel Plaza in New York*

*Jimmy Donahue with the Duke at Portofino, 1953*

was a cousin of Barbara Hutton. The Duchess was delighted by him, he made her laugh with his wise cracks and amused her very much. Donahue was well known to be homosexual, he was also nineteen years younger than she: he was thus considered by her to be a perfectly suitable escort. She liked sitting up late and the Duke did not; often, whether in New York or Paris, he went home to bed and she stayed on at some party laughing with Jimmy Donahue. The Duke got tired of the sight of Jimmy Donahue, and for a while there was the nearest thing to a rift between the devoted couple that they ever had in their thirty-five years of marriage. When the Duchess saw that the Duke really disliked him she stopped seeing Donahue. Someone asked in 1954: 'Do you still see so much of the Duchess of Windsor?' and Donahue replied: 'No. I've abdicated.'

Shortly after this episode Gaston Palewski was dining with the Windsors and the Duke said: 'This is our wedding day. We've been married eighteen years. There *may* be a happier couple somewhere, but I doubt it.'

# XVIII
## *The Brilliant Duchess*

A land where even the old are fair
And even the wise are merry of tongue.

*Yeats*

The Duchess of Windsor was always on the list of the 'best-dressed women in the world,' but she did not buy large numbers of dresses. She went to excellent dressmakers in Paris and wore her clothes for years. After Mainbocher, she got most of her clothes from Balenciaga, and some from Dior and Déssès. In his day, Balenciaga was the greatest and most imaginative dressmaker in the world, a true artist. He liked making things for the Duchess. Dior, where she is spoken of affectionately, invented a blue for her. It was not Wallis blue, but a dark purple blue which set off her dark colouring and deep blue eyes. Déssès, like Mainbocher of old, made very plain, well-cut clothes, which could be worn for years. When Balenciaga retired, Hubert de Givenchy started making for the Duchess, and he asked Balenciaga: 'Cristobal, may I copy your idea of an *housse* in Wallis blue for the Duchess with her name embroidered on it?' Balenciaga said: '*Mais bien sûr!*' and it was in that *housse* that dresses went for fittings in the house in the Bois de Boulogne. It is a dress cover made of linen in what the French call *le bleu Wallis* and embroidered in white: '*SAR [Son Altesse Royale] la Duchesse de Windsor.*'

People who worked for the Duchess nearly always became fond of her, and Hubert de Givenchy is no exception. From the point of view of a great *couturier* she was an ideal client, partly because of her fashionable measurements – 34-24-34 – even more because of the care she took about every detail from shoes to jewellery, and above all for her sure taste. Givenchy says that when it was rumoured that he was to make her dresses he was told (by people who did not know her) that the Duchess never paid her bills; in fact, he found that she paid them on the dot. He treasures in his memory a vision of extreme elegance: the Duchess of Windsor, standing in a window at the seventeenth-century Hotel Lambert on

*Previous page: Horst's photograph of the Duchess amid flowers in her drawing room in Paris*

*Above: One of Horst's portraits of the Duchess taken in the early 1950s*

190

the Ile St-Louis wearing a yellow dress made by Balenciaga and jewels to match.

Quite apart from anything else, all this would have been a positive drawback for her in England. Not since Queen Elizabeth I, with a dress for every day of the year, many of them embroidered with gems, has there been a queen who was the glass of fashion. The English possibly prefer a royal family dressed in gumboots and head scarves, with sparkling bejewelled tulle for great occasions. The Duchess never wore gumboots. She was a *femme d'intérieur*. When she and the Duke went to London at the invitation of the Queen to attend the unveiling of a plaque to Queen Mary and she was photographed with the royal family, the Duchess in her Paris clothes looked like the denizen of another planet, among the flowery toques and pastel overcoats.

She could hardly have been more unlike an English country lady. She did not care for games with the exception of poker and bridge, let alone for sport, fishing, shooting or hunting. She liked flowers but not gardening. Agriculture passed her by.* Her only exercise was dancing, or a short stroll with the pugs. She paid great attention to her appearance with constant hairdressing, massage and other beauty aids. She was not much of a reader, except of newspapers and magazines. The biographies and history books, of which we heard in the early days of her marriage at La Croë, had long since been abandoned, and novels and whodunits filled sleepless hours at night. Fortunately she did not care for music; the Duke would have suffered if she had. She preferred little pastiche 'furniture pictures' to great art. In most of these ways she resembled former queens far more than she did the English or Scotch aristocracy, which down the ages has been so fond of sport while at the same time collecting the very best French furniture and art from all over Europe.

The Duchess liked company, amusing conversation, parties, and a very little excellent food and wine. She liked what was new, particularly new fashions as long as they were in the classic tradition and she admired perfection in workmanship. If she saw china or glass that she thought pretty at a Palm Beach picnic she ordered crates to go to the Mill, so that guests were sometimes surprised to be given a noble ancient claret in thick green glasses or to eat with tin knives and forks with bamboo handles, just for a change. She liked to feel up-to-date, *à la page*. 'I'm sure *you've* never *heard* of Liberace,' she said once accusingly to the author, when Liberace and his candelabra and his sparkling suit had had a lot of publicity.

*As it did Queen Mary, who in her eighties, astonished country people by saying: 'So *that's* what hay looks like'.

What she meant was: 'You don't read the popular papers.' Another time she said: 'You're lucky. The Dook* and I have no children, but your sons bring young people to your house.' She liked the idea of 'young people'.

An American friend of hers is on record as having said: 'The trouble with Wallis is she's never done anything but keep house.' If this means she never composed a symphony or painted a masterpiece, it is of course true. A perfect dinner and brilliant talk in a delightful setting is as ephemeral as an unrecorded song, but it can nevertheless be a minor work of art, just as dressmaking can be. She kept house supremely well, her own appearance was supremely elegant; she was 'a wonderful wife to the Duke', in the words of the second Lord Monckton, son of the Windsors' great friend Walter. He adds: 'The one thing I remember about the Duchess is the extraordinary gift she had, so pleasing to men, in that she quickly found out what one's interests were, and they were immediately hers for the next ten minutes. I always found her charming, kind.'** This was not an act. She really was interested by people, their point of view, their work, their ambitions and likes and dislikes.

Why were her parties such a success? Delicious food and wine and comfort go a long way, but not the whole way. The Duchess was an excellent hostess, none of her guests felt left out, she encouraged talk. (Cole Porter said it was like a good rally at tennis with her, she always returned the ball.) She invited clever men of various nationalities but principally French, American and English, journalists, politicians, writers, doctors; and beautiful, chic women. The Duke remained, as he had always been, a fascinator. She noticed in a second if someone was boring him and moved everyone round. Ignoring protocol, she put English guests near him so that they could talk about old friends from the past.

The Duke and the Duchess each kept half an eye on the other, she to be sure all was well, he because she was the only person he was really interested in. One day when he had half heard something she said he called down the table: 'Darling! Did I hear you say Queen Mary?' 'Yes. But it wasn't *your* Queen Mary. We're talking about *Bloody* Mary,' was the reply.

On one occasion at the Mill the table was decorated with hundreds of yellow pansies. A guest said to the Duke: 'Oh, Sir, I'd no idea you were so fond of pansies'. She was rewarded by an icy stare, it was the sort of joke he disliked.

A journalist they both liked was Kenneth Harris, who did an

*The Duchess pronounced duke in the American way, and so, towards the end of his life, did the Duke himself.

**In a letter to the author.

*Above: Paris fashion amongst the toques: the Duchess of Windsor watches the Duke kissing the Queen Mother at the unveiling of a plaque to Queen Mary*

*Overleaf: The Duchess in 1959*

interview with them for English television. If any proof were needed that the Duke was not forgotten in Britain this appearance on television provided it. Instead of the usual audience of three or four million for Kenneth Harris's interviews with world celebrities, the night he was shown with the Windsors there were twelve million. The Duke was, and he would always remain, a folk legend in the land of his birth and his devotees seized this opportunity of getting to know the woman he loved.

The theory that the Windsors were 'bitter' is quite simply untrue. During the very first years the Duke felt frustrated and he was probably bitter about his war job. But after the war a period of great happiness began for them. Just as it would be hard to find two elderly people who loved each other and suited each other as well as they, so it would be difficult to exaggerate their contentment. If they laughed about the 'establishment' (a word they liked using) it was in the kindest possible way, though with evident gusto. The Duke was thankful that it did not fall to his lot to preside over the unprecedented decline in British prestige, power and prosperity. He was well aware that he could have done nothing to halt it, but the pulling down of Union Jacks all over the world would not have come easily to him.

During the last twenty or twenty-five years of the Duke's life there was never any question of going back to England except for a short visit now and again, and this suited the Duchess. There was not only the old contentious question of her title, but also the enormous taxes they would have had to pay. The French never taxed them. His mother and his favourite brother, the Duke of Kent, were no more, and a younger generation had taken over; what was past was done.

Another bar was the fact that they could not have taken their pugs to and fro, as they always did to America. They hated leaving the pugs. One day a large, strange-looking mongrel followed the Duchess back when she had been in the Bois with her dogs; she adopted him, and he was as much loved as the others.

Whenever the Duke and Duchess, or the Duke alone, visited London Walter Monckton was always on the platform as the train came in, most faithful of friends. During the war he had given up the Bar and gone into politics; he several times held high office. He and his second wife Biddy were frequent guests at the Mill and in Paris, they brought all the political gossip from London.

A friend of the Windsors, the witty journalist Hervé Mille, was once asked by the Duchess to try to get the receipt of a delicious *chaud-froid de poulet* that she had enjoyed while staying at Mouton with the Philippe de Rothschilds. He did his best, and when they

*When the Duke arrived in London, he was always met by Lord Monckton: (above) the Duke acknowledging cheers from the crowd; (below) Monckton with the Duke and Duchess*

all dined together at the Windsors' he saw Baron Philippe de Rothschild take a sealed envelope out of his pocket and give it to the Duchess. Delighted, she opened it and read the following from Mme de Rothschild:

Madame,

I am infinitely sensible of the honour done me by your royal highness's interest in having the receipt of my *chaud-froid*. Nevertheless, great as is my respectful devotion, I cannot go as far as to cut off my arm. Yet without my hand, the receipt is useless, even to the most eminent chef.

Both the Duchess and Pauline de Rothschild were American born, but after many years in France they had acquired a certain attitude towards the high importance of receipts, dishes, wines. Great laughter greeted this firm refusal.

Hervé Mille speaks of the 'rapid, brilliant sallies' of the Duchess,* which were appreciated by her French friends. A rather hard brilliance is often associated with her, but she had a sentimental side. Walter Lees took a choir of carol singers to the house in the Bois for a surprise one Christmas Eve; she wrote to him: 'I can't begin to tell you how touched the Duke and I were with the Christmas carols you brought to us – I had tears in my eyes at times.' During the private showing of his documentary film *A King's Story* Jack Le Vien sat where he could see the Duke and Duchess, and a few tears fell. No wonder. It would have been an unimaginative person indeed who could see this film in the presence of its strange, unique subject, unmoved.

*In conversation with the author.

197

# XIX
## Old Age

Ungebeten und ungewarnt nimmt sie uns
in den Kreislauf ihres Tanzes auf, und
treibt sich mit uns fort, bis wir ermüdet
sind und ihrem Arme entfallen.

*Goethe*, 'Natur'.

'They are not long, the days of wine and roses . . .' For the Windsors, as for everyone else, they came to an end. One by one their friends died. The Duchess fought old age and illness every inch of the way, with characteristic determination and courage. In 1964 the Duke was operated on for a 'ballooning artery' by Dr de Bakey in Houston, Texas, who put a length of plastic inside him; he made a complete recovery. Dr and Mrs de Bakey became friends of the Windsors and were guests at the Mill whenever they went to France. Then the Duke was operated on for detached retina by Mr James Hudson at the London Clinic. Their general practitioner from New York, Dr Antenucci, flew over to be with the Windsors and was present at the operation. Mr Hudson was 'absolutely enchanted with the Duchess and her devotion during the Duke's time in hospital'.* She had a room next to his in the Clinic, sat with him all day and read the newspapers to him. When they were at Claridge's awaiting the operation Bruce Ogilvy went to see them, for the last time, and the Queen visited her uncle in hospital.

The Duke could now no longer work in his garden. When he had lumbago and could not stoop, the Duchess got him a wooden milking stool on which he sat to weed the borders, but now his sight was impaired. They put the Mill up for sale; it was essential to economize somewhere, but he missed the place. They asked too high a price and once, when a deal was almost completed, the whole thing was discussed in the gossip column of an English newspaper and the purchaser withdrew. The sale hung fire.

One evening the Windsors were dining in Paris with Princess Caetani; the Duke was playing gin rummy. He had become quite silent and his neighbour reminded him: 'Sir, it's your turn.' At

*In a letter to the author from Mrs Hudson.

*The Duchess and the Duke with Mr John Utter, the Duke's private secretary, after the Duke's operation for detached retina in 1965 at the London Clinic*

*Above: The Duchess as godmother to the son of Henry and Linda Mortimer in 1969. Linda is the daughter of Major 'Fruity' Metcalfe*

*Overleaf: The visit of Queen Elizabeth II, the Duke of Edinburgh and Prince Charles to the Windsors' Paris home in May 1972. The Duke was too ill to receive his family*

that moment the Duke, who seemed to be fast asleep, fell slowly off his chair. He was lifted onto a sofa, where after a few moments he recovered consciousness, saying: 'Where is my cigar?' A fellow-guest has described the tender solicitude shown by the Duchess and also her remarkable presence of mind when everyone else was inclined to panic. She opened her bag and found the doctor's telephone number, and made someone alert the American Hospital and her own house, saying she might be arriving with the Duke within a few minutes. In the event he quite recovered and they were able to go home.

Cora Caetani's maid, pale with emotion, stood at the bottom of the stairs when the Duke appeared, leaning on the Duchess's arm. Thinking she was a Spaniard he told her, in Spanish, how much he loved Spain. But she said she was Portuguese. 'Marvellous country,' said the Duke, unperturbed. 'I must say he was a model of pluck, dignity and courtesy,' says a witness of the scene.

Early in 1972 the Duke's old friend Lord Sefton was ill and the Duchess wrote a note of sympathy to 'Dearest Foxie', Lady Sefton. 'We are not well. I have a flood of nerves and the Duke is having X-ray for his throat,' she said. Later, the Duke had had thirty deep X-ray treatments and they had done him good, but she added 'I too from worry have a painful time with my old friend the ulcer,' and 'There is nothing to be said for growing old'. The only cheerful thing was that Grace Dudley had been to see them, 'great rush and full of pep'.

The Duchess wished they had put all the money they spent on the Mill into a house in the South of France where the climate was better. The Duke was far from well, the cold and damp of Paris did not help, and there could be no question of travelling to America. The Duchess never smoked, but the Duke had smoked all his life, cigarettes, pipes, cigars. Even now that he had cancer of the throat he lit a cigar after dinner. He never gave in to illness and insisted on coming down if there were people dining, almost to the very end. It cheered him to see friends, and he was as interested as ever in what was going on in the world. His voice was sometimes a whisper and sometimes quite loud and harsh, it seemed as if it must hurt him to talk, but he refused to give up.

When the Queen visited the Windsors in May 1972 the Duke was too ill to come downstairs to receive her. She sat with him in his room; she must have realized he was dying. A photograph was taken of the Queen, Prince Philip, Prince Charles and the Duchess on the steps of the house.

The Duke died on 28 May 1972, within a month of his seventy-

*Previous pages: The widowed Duchess with the Queen Mother after the Duke's funeral at St George's Chapel, Windsor*

*Above: The Duchess watching the return of the procession from Trooping the Colour, 'her face the very image of grief'. During the ceremony, the pipers played 'The Flowers of the Forest' as a lament for the Duke*

eighth birthday. With each news bulletin the BBC broadcast his Abdication speech; it made the same impact as it had thirty-five years before. His body was flown to England in a RAF plane; the Duchess followed two days later in one of the Queen's aeroplanes. She was accompanied by Lady Soames, Grace Lady Dudley, Dr Antenucci and Mr John Utter, the Duke's private secretary. She no longer feared flying, she felt her life was over.

Her friend Hubert de Givenchy had given her some mourning dresses and his tailors made her a black coat in a single night, a feat unparalleled in the annals of *haute couture.* The Queen invited her to stay at Buckingham Palace, and Grace Dudley looked after the Duchess. While she was there the ceremony of Trooping the Colour took place. The Queen wore a black arm-band on her uniform and pipers played 'The Flowers of the Forest', a lament for the Duke. The Duchess looked out of a window at the Palace, her face the very image of grief.

The lying-in-state was in St George's Chapel, Windsor, and the night before the funeral Prince Charles motored the Duchess down after the crowds had gone. Perhaps it was a surprise to the authorities that there were crowds, perhaps they believed the Duke had been forgotten. After all, it was more than thirty-five years since the Abdication. Sixty thousand people made the journey to Windsor to pay their respects to the King who had reigned for eleven months so long ago, to the Prince of Wales who had been and would always remain a folk legend.

He was buried near Queen Victoria and Prince Albert in the family Mausoleum at Frogmore. After the funeral the Duchess flew back to France, and the photograph of this tiny figure in black going up the steps of the aeroplane alone seemed for many people to underline the terrible loneliness that would now begin for her. To get back to the empty house; never more to be greeted by the Duke's call: 'Darling, darling, I'm here!' He had cherished, adored and protected her for nearly four decades with his extraordinary devotion. There can hardly ever have been a widow with quite so much to miss as she.

The Duchess had no relations but many friends, and her friends tried to help. After the first shock of grief she saw them often, but she was often tired and depressed, unhappy and lonely. After a time, to escape from this, she began going out too much; but it made her worse. 'Try to learn to say no,' her doctor told her.

In the spring of 1974 she went to America, sailing on the southern route in the *SS Raffaello*, but she soon came back to France, saying she was 'homesick'. She looked upon France as home, and often said: 'France has been very good to us.' That summer the Duchess

*Above: The Duchess returning to France, alone, after the funeral of the Duke, 5 June 1972*

*Left: A dinner party given by the Duchess in Paris in 1975. From the left, Mme de Heeren, Princess von Bismarck, the Duchess, the author (back to camera)*

flew to England in one of the Queen's aeroplanes, visited the Duke's grave, and went home the same day.

Her servants were devoted to her, and there she had great good fortune. The perfect French butler, Georges, and his wife Ofélia, were real friends and they were the linchpin of the household. The excellent cook stayed on, until the time came when only invalid food was required. When he was asked why, he said it was because he learned so much from the Duchess. The loyalty of her household after the Duke's death was admirable.

Her own illness began with a broken leg; she got over this fairly quickly, but on 13 November 1975 she had a haemorrhage, and from then on was never quite well again. At times she seemed to be on the point of recovery, but it always eluded her, and her many friends could do little to help.

Her lawyer, the clever and devoted Maître Suzanne Blum, looked after her interests eagle-eyed. Once, when the Duchess was carried downstairs to her *chaise longue* on the terrace a photographer with a long-distance lens got a picture of her which was published in various newspapers and on French television. Maître Blum sued on her behalf, and each paper was obliged to pay more than £8,000 damages. It was an invasion of privacy, a serious matter in France.

The French admired the Duchess, not only her friends but the public in general. A few years after the Duke's death a film about the Abdication was shown on French television called *The Woman he Loved*. It was followed by a discussion in the studio; friends of hers taking part included M. Maurice Schumann and Lord Tennyson, and there were others, Professor Hugh Thomas the historian among them. The part of the Duchess was acted by Fay Dunaway who succeeded in looking exactly like her. (The Duke is quite impossible to act, it is hard to say why. Perhaps it is because no actor can simulate his royal aura.) During the subsequent discussion members of the public could telephone to ask questions or give their point of view. The questions were all on the lines of 'How many times has the Duchess been invited to Buckingham [French for Buckingham Palace]?' There was a good deal of criticism of her treatment by the Duke's country, and this fairly represents the French point of view. She had lived so long in France and she had so obviously made the Duke happy that people there failed to understand why this was not universally recognized.

Possibly his happiness was the trouble. There had never been, in the words of the lady who wrote long ago to Victor Cazalet, 'a fearful awakening'.

In 1978 a television serial, *Edward and Mrs Simpson*, was shown in Britain. When the Duchess asked to see the script, it was not forthcoming. It was announced in the press that she objected to this invasion of her privacy, and it did indeed seem an extraordinarily tasteless way to behave to a widow who was old and known to be far from well. The result was a flood of letters of sympathy from all over Britain to the Duchess, of which the following extracts are typical.

'Thousands of British people, like ourselves, are outraged at this intrusion.'

'There are thousands of British people who love you very much.'

'Many ordinary people such as myself and many of those with whom I work are disturbed, it seems to us to be a gross intrusion of your privacy.'

'You are a wonderful lady, with great dignity.'

'I shall always admire the late Duke. I shall remember him *always* as a great man.'

'I love you both for what you did and if only more people were like you the world would be a happier place.'

'. . . great love and admiration for a very great lady.'

'You see, dear, he didn't turn his back on the working people and this is why he was so well liked, and you yourself were a loving person whom we all love. The people wanted you, Mr Baldwin didn't. How wrong he was.'

'I would like you to be aware that the majority of British people are much saddened by the present television series.'

'. . . disgust at the recent TV show. To hundreds of working-class people the late *King* was their much-loved King and your marriage a true love match.'

'A love story such as yours is something precious.'

'I feel ashamed.'

'. . . I have not watched it, on principle.'

'I feel so great a love as your Royal Highness has known can only be envied and admired by so many.'

'The British Legion was behind him to a man. Winston Churchill was his staunch friend and it is a pity he is not here to defend him.'

There is no doubt that letters such as these, which arrive in sheaves, are balm to the Duchess as she lies in her room at the house in the Bois, or sometimes in the American Hospital at Neuilly.

Georges and Ofélia care for her. A friend who left some flowers, saddened by the atmosphere in what had formerly been a house full of laughter and gaiety, asked whether anyone spoke to the Duchess about the years when she was so greatly loved. Georges replied: '*Oui. Je lui parle souvent du passé.*'

The last time the author went to sit with the Duchess, her face looked like the Greek mask of tragedy, her mouth a square, her dark and penetrating blue eyes staring out of the window. There is nothing to be said for growing old, as she herself wrote, and where there is deep love between two people there is nothing to be said for being the one who is left alone.

## XX
# Summing Up

There are two things to aim at in life;
first, to get what you want; and after that,
to enjoy it. Only the wisest of mankind
achieve the second.

*Logan Pearsall Smith*

The Duchess of Windsor's story is unique. A novel describing such a strange life as hers would hardly find a publisher, the truth altogether too bizarre even for fiction. This may be one reason why she has so often been attacked; people dislike what they cannot understand, and the Windsors' history does not fit into any of the customary stereotypes of human behaviour. Even more than the Abdication, the life-long devotion and adoration she received from the Duke surprises many and exasperates some, and since this obviously lay deep within his character, the most that can be done is to attempt to understand him.

But the Abdication itself remains for many people something of a mystery. The King's insistence that he must marry Mrs Simpson was, as we have seen, enough in itself to make it inevitable, but could it really have been the only reason? Some believe in a hidden hand, a plot by politicians to eliminate the King, perhaps because he was loved in such a very special way by the ordinary people and ex-servicemen, which potentially gave him power no king should possess. Some believe they got rid of him because he wanted peace with Germany (yet one of his ardent supporters was Churchill, the man of war). Others again thought the King himself felt his impotence in everything that mattered to his country was so inhibiting that he preferred to go. There may or may not be a grain of truth in all these things. Thirty years after the Abdication the Duke of Windsor wrote in 1966 in the *New York Daily News:* 'Being a monarch . . . in these egalitarian times can surely be one of the most confining, the most frustrating, and over the duller stretches the least stimulating jobs open to an educated, independent-minded person.' He probably thought that the Duke of York would be a more successful King than he, which, as we know, is what their father George v himself thought.

*Wallis and the King during one of the happiest times of their life: relaxing among sightseers on the Dalmatian Coast, during the cruise of the* Nahlin *in 1936*

When the royal princes were on the threshold of manhood King George V's old friend Lord Derby, with whom he was staying at Knowsley, made some observations about the relations between fathers and sons. He was distressed by the King's hectoring tone with his children. He told him how much he enjoyed the company of his own sons now that they were grown up, and hinted that if he stopped bullying the King also might find pleasure in the company of the princes. George V was silent for a long moment, then he said: 'My father was frightened of his mother, I was frightened of my father, and I am going to make damned sure my sons are frightened of me.' This Mr Pontifex-like observation left Lord Derby with no possible rejoinder. There is a certain pathos about such a desire to dominate and crush; only a weak man could have spoken thus. The King was delicate, and often ill.

The trouble really began when the Prince of Wales grew out of being frightened of his father. He was liberated by the war, and by the fact of his own overwhelming popularity. The King went on with his scoldings but the Prince paid no attention, even when traps were laid for him about matters the King thought very important, like orders and decorations. Lady Airlie, who saw all this going on year after year, admired the Prince's forbearance, and never was it more admirable than when much later, as Duke of Windsor, he wrote his memoirs. He referred to his father's private war with the twentieth century, but there is not a word of criticism, let alone an account of the old King's strange behaviour to 'dear David', as he called his heir.

At the time, however, the Prince took good care to ration his visits to Balmoral and Sandringham to a minimum; he had a strong desire not to put too great a strain upon whatever fragile ties of family affection remained. One of 'David's fads', with which it is easy to sympathize, is that he chose to enjoy his free time as far away as possible from the denizens of Buckingham Palace, and that he chose his friends and his lovers among people as unlike his parents and his father's friends as he could find. He must have resolved never himself to be in any way like his father and, insofar as George V was considered an excellent King, it is possible that he doubted whether he was the man for the job.

He may have thought to himself: 'Here am I, forbidden to make even suggestions about matters of life and death for the country; would not the English establishment be better off with someone who could take a genuine interest in orders and decorations and so forth?' He probably half guessed about his father's passionate prayer that nothing should come between the Duke of York and the throne.

*Previous page: The Duke and Duchess on their wedding day at Candé, 1937*

*Above: The Duke and Duchess on board their yacht at Portofino, 1955*

In a recent biography\* there is a reference to 'the terrible responsibilities of the role he inherited'. It would be interesting to know what these terrible responsibilities are supposed to have been. Nobody, not even a republican (if such a person exists in Britain, which is doubtful) would dream of blaming the Sovereign for the steady decline of our country during the last thirty years. The terrible responsibility for that belongs to the politicians.

Nevertheless, though powerless in a political sense, the Sovereign and the royal family are important to Britain, and not only because of tradition. There is more to it than jubilees, coronations and weddings, though exactly what this may be is not easy to define. A contemporary French Catholic priest, Father Jean-Maria Charles-Roux, has put forward his idea of where this importance lies in his book, *Mon Dieu et Mon Roi;* the following is a rough translation:

> The State is symbolized by a family which is part of the country's history. Every manifestation of official life, whether in the capital or in the provinces, is an opportunity for a member of this family to be present, a prince, a princess, the King, the Queen, representing everyone's uncle or cousin or child or parent.
>
> In the councils of the State the presence of someone entirely unpolitical but with a heart, a conscience, a spirit, is of inestimable value in the evolution of society.

This, together with grand and beautiful ceremonies, seems to be about the measure of it. That there is nothing here about terrible responsibilities in no way detracts from the importance of the role played by the royal family and above all by the Monarch. Provided there is continuity, it is perhaps rather exaggerated to make too much play with 'duty' and 'responsibility'. At the time of the Abdication the King had three brothers, each with a wife eminently suitable to be queen. Continuity was assured.

The Duchess of Windsor was told at her wedding by Walter Monckton that she must try to make the Duke happy 'all his days'. Her triumph is that she did so. When they were in the Bahamas she sent a letter by hand to Queen Mary describing the Duke's life and his activities; it was taken by a bishop who was leaving for England. Queen Mary did not reply, but next time she wrote to the Duke she sent 'a kind message to your wife', which surprised him, since he knew nothing of the Duchess's letter. In 1951 the Duchess was ill in New York and Queen Mary hoped she was getting better. Otherwise nothing. It is easy to understand why it was Queen Mary who most resented the Abdication; she announced

\**Edward VIII* by Frances Donaldson

that she felt 'humiliated' by it. She was imbued with a sense of the importance of being royal, and she never recovered from having been a Serene Highness among Royal Highnesses.

It must not be supposed that the Duchess of Windsor lost any sleep over this. The relationship is seldom an easy one, and many a daughter-in-law would be delighted with such loose ties between herself and her husband's family. The Duke was forty-three when he married, and none of his relations was important to him except his brother the Duke of Kent. Even he, since his own marriage, had ceased to be the close companion of former days. The Duchess completely filled the Duke's heart, and the idea that he hankered for his family is all of a piece with the theory that he was a sad exile. It has been invented by the people who were vainly waiting for the 'fearful awakening' that never came.

Perhaps it is over-optimistic to say that all ended very well, but that is how it seems. The royal family is as popular as ever, members of it marry anyone they fancy and nobody minds when a marriage ends, or begins, with a divorce. (If the Archbishops mind, they keep quiet about it.) The Duke of Windsor had thirty-five happy years with the Duchess. He is not forgotten, and neither is she. On anniversaries, her birthday, their wedding day, hundreds

*Wallis returns to Baltimore: the Duke and Duchess at the Sheraton-Belvedere Hotel in 1959*

of letters from well-wishers came from England; another proof that what is called 'a bad press' does not have quite the effect that might be imagined. The only sad thing is her long, long illness at the end of life.

When the Duke said to James Pope-Hennessy: 'I played fair in 1936 but I have been bloody shabbily treated', he did not mean that his offer of service to his country was rejected, that was up to the authorities. The notion that he was aching to lay a few more foundation stones, and that he was deeply offended not to be permitted to do it, hardly merits a moment's consideration. What he meant was that ordinary, common or garden good manners were lacking. It was something he found as hard to understand as to forgive, being himself the embodiment of what a French acquaintance described as an '*exquise courtoisie*'.

Speaking to a friend about ex-King Umberto of Italy, a footnote in history, the Duchess once said: 'Kings haven't much of a part to play nowadays; it's not Umberto's fault if he's forgotten', then, indicating the Duke who was out of earshot, she added: '*He* will be spoken of for a long time to come – because of *me*!'

She was perfectly right. As Winston Churchill said to Lady Airlie: 'The Duke's love for her is one of the great loves of history.'

# INDEX

Entries in *italics* refer to page numbers of pictures.

Abdication, 115-22; broadcast, 115, 119-22; instrument of, *120*; French film about, 209; reasons for, 212

Abdy, Jane, Lady, 154

Abertillery miners, *105*

Abyssinia, 90

Adenauer, Konrad, 162

Adolphus, Prince of Teck, 29, 30, 40

Aird, Major Jack, 81

Airlie, Mabell, Countess of, 34, 67, 84, 172

Albert, Prince, later George VI, *see* Bertie, Prince

Albert, Prince Consort, 31n, 32, 38

Albert Victor, Duke of Clarence, *see* Eddy, Prince

Alexander, Major Ulick, 122

Alexandra, Queen, 34

Allen, Alice Montague (*for earlier entries see* Warfield, Alice Montague), 53, 57

Allen, Charles Gordon, 53, *54*

Allen, George, 136

Aly Khan, 77

Annapolis Naval Academy, *60*

Antenucci, Dr, 198, 207

Asquith, H. H. (*later* Earl of Oxford), 32

Astor, Nancy, Viscountess, *72*, 89

Augusta, Grand-Duchess of Mecklenburg-Strelitz, 41

Bakey, Dr de, 198

Baldwin, Stanley, 96-8, *108*, 116, 118; first meeting with Wallis, 86; 'black beetle' car, *102*; and King's attitude to South Wales miners, 106; and morganatic marriage proposal, 107; and Abdication speech, 115; Commons address on Abdication, 119; and Beaverbrook, 122; on Abdication, 124

Balenciaga, 188

Beaton, Sir Cecil, 96, 136; photographs of Wallis, *10*, *152*

Beaverbrook, Lord, 98, 101, 107, *108*, 168n; and Baldwin, 122

Bedaux, Charles, 129, 148-9

Beistegui, Carlos de, 180-1

Benson, Lady (Rex), 129, 157

Berners, Lord, 86

Bertie, Prince (Duke of York) (*for later entries see* George VI), *35*, 39, 63

Biarritz, *80*

Bigelow, Katherine Moore (*for later entries see* Rogers, Katherine), 49-50

Birkenhead, 2nd Earl of, 122

Birkett, Norman, 98

Bismarck, Princess von, *208*

Blue Ridge Summit, 12, *14*

Blum, Maître Suzanne, 209

Boris, Tsar of Bulgaria, 94

Bowes-Lyon, Lady Elizabeth (*later* Queen Elizabeth), 70

Boyd Orr, Sir John, 106

Bradford, Bishop of, 109

Brandt, Willy, 162

Brownlow, Lady, 81, 85

Brownlow, Lord, 81, 85, *117*, 117-18, 119; takes Wallis to France, 109-14

Bryanston Court, 57, *69*, 77, 96

Brynmawr, 104

Buist, Colin, 85, *142*

Buist, Mrs, 85, 97, *142*

Cadogan, Major, 41, 45

Caetani, Princess, 198-201

Candé, Château de, 129, *130*, 136

Cannes, 53, 81

Carr, Raymond, 64

Cartier, Jacques, 150

Cavan, Major General (*later* Field-Marshal) Earl of, 45, 47

Cavendish, Lord Charles, 62

Cazalet, Victor, 116&n, 124

Chamberlain, Neville, 101, 140, 155

Chambrun, Comtesse René de, 153

Charles, Prince of Wales: visit to Windsors, *200*, 201

Charles-Roux, Father Jean-Maria, 217

Chatfield, Admiral Sir Ernle, 89

Chatfield, Lady, 89

China, 26, 49-50

Cholmondeley, Marquess of, 81

Christie, Sir Harold, 16

Churchill, Randolph, *134*, 136, 155, *156*

Churchill, (*later* Sir) Winston, 59, 89, 122, 155; admiration for Prince of Wales, 40; advice to Edward VIII, 107; attacks Baldwin, 115; and Abdication broadcast, 119; opposition to Munich settlement, 154; and treatment of Wallis, 161; address to Congress, 167; on Duke of Windsor, 172, 219

Clarence, Duke of, *see* Eddy, Prince

Colefax, Sir Arthur, 86

Colefax, Lady, 89, 90, 101, 129, 155

*Colis du Trianon, Les,* 157

Colyton, Lord, 26

Cooper, Lady Diana, 86, 89, 94
Cooper, Duff, 85, 86, 107, 154
Coote, Sir Colin, 47
Coward, Sir Noël, 157
Croë, Château de la, 143, *151*, 154, 172
Cromer, 2nd Earl of, 58
Cunard, Lady, 86, 90

Derby, 17th Earl of, 214
Dessès, 188
Devonshire, Evelyn, Duchess of, 62&n, 67
Dior, 188
Divorce laws, 98
Dodds, Major, 160
Donahue, Jimmy, 183-7, *186*
Dudley, Grace, Countess of, 180, 201, 207
Dudley, Earl of, 140, 180
Dunaway, Fay, 209

Eddy, Prince (Prince Albert Victor, Duke of Clarence), 29, 30-1
Eden, Anthony, 85, 154
Edinburgh, Philip, Duke of: visit to Windsors, *200*, 201
Edward VII; as Prince of Wales, 29, 30; as King, 38, 81
Edward VIII (*for earlier entries see* Edward, Prince, and Edward, Prince of Wales; *for later entries see* Windsor, Duke of), *87*, *88*; Accession, 85, *87*; at Pompeii, *92*; cruise on *Nahlin*, 94; entertaining at Balmoral, 97; speech from Throne, 98; after State Opening of Parliament (1936), *99*; visits South Wales, 104, *105*; popularity, 106; Abdication broadcast, 115, 119-22, *120*; instrument of Abdication, *120*; after Abdication broadcast, *120*
Edward, Prince (*for later entries see* Edward, Prince of Wales; Edward VIII; Windsor, Duke of), *35*, *42*, *43*, *46*, *59*; birth, 32; christening, 34; childhood, 34-9
Edward, Prince of Wales (*for later entries see* Edward VIII; Windsor, Duke of) relations with his father, 38-9, 62, 70-3, 84, 214; becomes Prince of Wales, 40, *42*; at Oxford, 41; commission in Grenadiers, 44; in Khartoum, 47; in Italy, 47; Lord Cavan's report on him, 47; popularity, 58, 70; American visit (1919), *60*, 61; tours of Empire, 58-62; life in London, 62-4; fox hunting, 64; steeple-chasing, *66*; in America (1924), 67; first meeting with Wallis, 69; relations with his mother, 69-70; playing bagpipes, *72*; acquires Fort Belvedere, 74; at Fort Belvedere, *75*; rumours of romance

with Wallis, 78; skiing at Kitzbühl, 79, *80*; at Biarritz, *80*
*Edward and Mrs Simpson* (television serial), 209-10
Elizabeth II: visits Duke in hospital, 198; visit to Windsors in France, *200*, 201
Elizabeth, Queen Mother, 70, *206* equerries, 63&n
Esher, 2nd Viscount, 40, 58
Espil, Don Felipe, 24, *25*
Espirito Santo, Senhor, 161

Fellowes, the Hon. Mrs Reginald, 81, 129
Fisher, Admiral Sir William, 122
Fitzgerald, Evelyn, *93*
Fitzgerald, Mrs, *76*, *93*
Fort Belvedere, 69, 74, *75*, *76*; entertaining at, 85-6
Forwood, Sir Dudley, 136, 140, *142*, *145*
Franz Ferdinand, Archduke, 41, 44, 107
Frederick, Empress, 29, 32, 34
Frederick II, King of Prussia, 39
Frederick William, King of Prussia, 39
Furness, Thelma, Lady, 69, *71*, *76*, 77, 78

Gaulle, General Charles de, 169
George V (*for earlier entries see* George, Prince), 40, 46; Accession, 38; hobbies, 38; relations with Prince of Wales, 38-9, 62, 70-3, 84, 214; Silver Jubilee, 81, *82*; death, 84
George VI (*for earlier entries see* Bertie, Prince), 32; and Duke of Windsor, 143, 149; funeral, 172
George, Prince, Duke of York (*for later entries see* George V), *28*, 29-30, 31, 32, 38
George, Prince (*later* Duke of Kent), 62, 69, 79, 195, 218
Germany, Windsors' pre-war visit to, 143-8
Givenchy, Hubert de, 188-200, 207
Goddard, Theodore, 89, 96, *97*, 98, 118
Gordon, General 'Chinese', 47
Gordon-Lennox, Lady Algernon, 84
Greece, King of, 93
Goering, General, 144
Guinness, Mrs Kenelm, 78
Gwynne, 'Foxie' (*later* Countess of Sefton), 85, *142*, 201

Haig, General Sir Douglas, 45
Halifax, Countess of, 167
Halifax, Earl of, 167
Halsey, Admiral, 61
Hamilton, Lord Claud, 63
Hansell, Mr (royal tutor), 41

Hardie, Keir, 34
Hardinge, the Hon. Alexander, *later* 2nd Lord Hardinge of Penshurst, 100
Harmsworth, the Hon. Esmond, *97*, 98, 107
Harris, Kenneth, 192, 195
Heeren, Mme de, *208*
Hélène, Princess of Orléans, 29
Henry, Prince, *35*
Henry, Prince of Prussia, 44
Hitler, Adolf, 144, *147*, 154
Hoare, Lady Maud, 89
Hoare, Sir Samuel, 89, 90, 161
Hoare-Laval Pact, 90
Hohenberg, Duchess of, 41
Housing: in pre-war Britain, 143, 144; low cost, in Germany, 144
Howard-Vyse, Major-General Sir Richard, 157, 160
Hudson, James, F.R.C.S., 198
Hudson, Mrs James, 198
Hunter, Mr & Mrs George, 98

India, 61-2

James, Admiral Sir William, 155
Jardine, Reverend Anderson, *134*, 136; prayerbook, *135*
Jowitt, Sir William, 138

*Kelly, HMS*, *156*
Kemal, Mustapha, 94
Kent, Duke of (Prince George), 62, 69, 79, 195, 218
Khartoum, 45-7
Kirk, Mary (*for later entries see* Raffray), *20*, 21
Kirkwood, Dr, 118-9
Kitchener, Earl, 44-5
Kitzbühl, 79, *80*

Ladbroke (the chauffeur), 113
Lang, Cosmo, Archbishop of Canterbury, 84, *123*; sermon castigating former King, 122-3
Lascelles, Viscount, 63
Lascelles, Sir Alan, 63, 94
Laval, Pierre, 153
Lees, Walter, 180, 197
Legh, Captain, the Hon. Piers, 63, 122
Le Vien, Jack, 183, *184*, 197
Ley, Dr, 144, *145*
Liberace, 191
Lindbergh, Charles, 86, 89, 154
Lindbergh, Mrs, 154
Lindsay, Sir Ronald, 149
Lipton, Sir Thomas, 70
Little, Colonel Louis, 49
Lloyd George, D., 40, 58, 115-6, 144, 148

Lloyd Thomas, Hugh, *76*, 136
Londonderry, 7th Marquess of, 144
Loú Viei, Villa, 53, 113, *117*; 127
Lucinge, Prince Jean-Louis de Faucigny, 157

McCulloh, Nan, 13
Mainbocher, 136, 154, 188
Margesson, David, 89
Marina, Princess of Greece, later Duchess of Kent, 79
Mary, Queen (*for earlier entries see* May, Princess), 39, 40, 103, 191n; dress, 55; relations with the Prince of Wales, 69-70; and Abdication broadcast, 119; funeral, 172; unveiling of plaque to, *193*; resentment of Abdication, 217
Mary, Princess, *35*, 39, 63
Mary Adelaide, Duchess of Teck, 29
Maugham, Somerset, 129
May, Princess (*for later entries see* Mary, Queen), 29, 30, 31n, 31-2, 34
Mendl, Sir Charles, 157
Mendl, Lady, 157
Merryman, Bessie (Wallis' aunt), 21, 57, 79, *99*, *134*, 167; opposition to divorce, 23; takes Wallis to London (1927), 53; as Wallis' chaperon, 78, 98; at Wallis' wedding to Duke, 138
Metcalfe, Lady Alexandra, *126*, 136
Metcalfe, Major 'Fruity', 62, *126*, *133*, *134*, *156*, *200*; on Duke's 'stinginess', 125; as best man, 136; as Duke's A.D.C., 157, 160
Mill, the (Moulin de la Tuilerie), 175-9, *176*; Duke's garden, 175, *176*
Mille, Hervé, 195, 197
Monarchy, popularity of, 81, 217
Monckton, Walter, later Viscount Monckton of Brenchley, 116, *117*, 122, *142*, 154-5, *196*; becomes King's adviser, 100; and Abdication speech, 119; anger at Archbishop's attack, 129; at Windsors' wedding, *134*, 139; on Wallis' right to title of Royal Highness, 138; as adviser to George VI, 143; visits to Mill, 195
Monckton, 2nd Viscount, 192
Monckton, Viscountess Bridget, 195
Montague, family name of Wallis' mother (*see* Warfield, Alice Montague *and* Allen, Alice Montague)
Moran, Lord, 167
Morganatic marriage, 29, 107
Morrison, Herbert, 144
Mortimer, Henry, *200*
Mortimer, Linda, *200*
Mountbatten, Lord Louis, 86, *97*, 155, *156*
Mountbatten, Lady Louis, *97*

Moyne, 1st Lord, 78
Munich settlement, 154
Munster, Count Paul, 140
Mustin, Captain, 19
Mustin (later Murray), Corinne, 19, 26, 68

Nahlin, cruise in, 92-3, 94
Nassau, 163, 164
Nicolson, Sir Harold, 33, 90, 155

Oakes, Sir Harry, 165, 167-8
O'Brien, Olive, 79, 80
Ogilvy, Captain the Honourable Bruce, 61, 63, 64, 67, 80, 127, 198
Ogilvy, the Hon. Mrs Bruce, 80
Oldfields school, 13, 17
Ormerod, Sir Berkeley, 181
Ormerod, Lady, 181
Oxford and Asquith, Margot, Countess of, 90

Page, Russell, 175
Palewski, Gaston, 169, 187
Paul, Prince of Jugoslavia, 95
Peacock, Sir Edward, 116
Peking, 49-50, 52
Pensacola, 19, 22
Philip, Prince, see Edinburgh, Duke of
Phillips, Major Gray, 160, 165
Point, Madame, 113
Pompeii, 92
Pope-Hennessy, James, 183, 219
Porter, Cole, 64, 192
Portofino, 186

Raffray, Captain Jacques, 21
Raffray, Mary (for earlier entries see Kirk), 53, 89, 128
Rasin, J. F., 12
Reboux, 136
Reith, Sir John, 119
Rivera, Miguel Primo de, 161
Rogers, Herman, 49-50, 53, 117, 128, 133, 136, 167
Rogers, Katherine (for earlier entries see Bigelow), 92, 97, 109, 117, 128; in Peking, 49-50; at Lou Viei, 53; at White House, 167
Roosevelt, President, 162, 167
Rosaura, the, 78
Rothschild, Baron Eugen, 122
Rothschild, Baronne Philippe de, 195-7
Rowntree, Seebohm, 106

Salisbury, Alice, Marchioness of, 61
San Diego, 22-3
Sanègre, Georges and Ofélia, 209, 210
Saxe-Coburg and Gotha, Duke of, 144
Schmidt, Paul, interpreter, 144, 148

Schumann, Maurice, 136, 209
Sebastian, Georges, 50, 175
Sefton, Countess of (formerly 'Foxie' Gwynne), 85, 142, 201
Sefton, Earl of, 81, 201
Selby, Lady, 136
Selby, Sir Walford, 161
Shanghai, 51
Sherriffe, Monica, 64
Sidney (Windsors' footman), 178
Sigrist, Frederick, 163
Simpson, Ernest, 56, 73, 89; early acquaintance with Wallis, 53; marriage to Wallis, 55; life in London, 57; at Fort Belvedere, 74; letter to Wallis after Abdication, 127
Simpson, Wallis (for earlier entries see Warfield; Spencer; for later entries see Windsor, Duchess of), 91; marriage, 55; first meeting with Prince of Wales, 69; presented at Court, 71; presented to Queen Mary, 79; skiing at Kitzbühl, 79, 80; at Pompeii, 92; cruise on Nahlin, 94; divorce petition, 95, 98; entertaining at Balmoral, 97; dash across France, 109-14, 115; in Cannes, 117; press statement before Abdication, 118; anonymous letters after Abdication, 127-8; at Château de Candé, 130; reunion with Duke at Candé, 132; marriage to Duke, 133-4, 136-9
Sister Anne, the, 81
Sitwell, Sir Osbert, 128-9
Smiley, Mrs Kerr, 55
Smith, Sydney, 172
Soames, the Hon. Lady, 207
Soixante gourmets, les, 24
Sopwith, Sir Thomas, 163
Spencer, Lieutenant Earl Winfield, 19-24; 20, 26, 50
Spencer, Wallis (for earlier entries see Warfield; for later entries see Simpson; Windsor, Duchess of): honeymoon, 21; in Washington, 24-6; in Coronado, 25; in Paris, 26; in China, 49-50; at Warrenton, 50; selling tubular steel, 53; divorce, 53; marriage to Ernest Simpson, 56
Spry, Constance, 134, 136
Squantum, Massachusetts, 22
Stamfordham, Lord, 44, 45
Sylvester, A. J., 116

Teck, Duchess of, 34
Teck, Duke of, 30, 31
Teck, Princess May of, see May, Princess
Tennyson, 4th Lord, 209
Thaw, Benjamin, 68, 69
Thomas, Sir Geoffrey, 63, 94

Thomas, Professor Hugh, 209
Trotter, Brigadier General 'G', 69, 74;
sacked by Prince of Wales, 78

Umberto, King of Italy, 219
Utter, John, *199*, 207

Vanderbilt, Mrs (Gloria), 68, 77
Venice, 180-1
Victoria, Queen, *28*, 29, 30, 31, 32;
and Edward VII, 38; popularity, 81

Wales, Prince of (Prince Edward), *see*
Edward, Prince of Wales
Wales, Princess Maud of (later Queen
of Norway), 30
Wallace, Mrs Euan (*later* Mrs Herbert
Agar), *76*, 85
Wallace, Euan, *76*, 85
Ward, Mrs Dudley, 64, *65*, 67
Wardell, Captain, Mike, 64
Warfield, Mrs (Wallis' grandmother),
*16*, 19
Warfield (*later* Allen), Alice Montague
(Wallis' mother), 12, *15*, *53*, *54*
Warfield, Governor Edwin, 12
Warfield, General Henry, 167
Warfield, Solomon (Wallis' uncle),
13, 23, 24, 26, 53
Warfield, Teackle Wallis (Wallis'
father), 12, *14*
Warfield, Wallis (*for later entries see*
Spencer; Simpson, Windsor,
Duchess of): birth, 12; family
background, 12-13; education, 13;
as debutante, 13, *18*; as schoolgirl, *16*;
marriage to Winfield Spencer, *20*, 21
Warrenton, 50
Washington, 24-6
Wasserleonburg, 140, *142*
Wells, H. G., 155
Westminster, 2nd Duke of, 81, 125, 161
William II, Emperor (the Kaiser), 41
Willingdon, the Marquess and
Marchioness of, 89

Windsor, Duchess of (*for earlier entries
see* Warfield; Spencer; Simpson):
denied title of Royal Highness, 138;
honeymoon, 140, *142*; in Germany
(1937), 144-5, *145*, *147*; superstitions,
150; clothes and jewellery, 150, 154,
188-91; life at La Croë, 150-3; Paris
house, 153, 154; on *HMS Kelly*, *156*;
war work in France, 157-60; in
French Womens' Ambulance Corps,
*159*; leaves France for Spain, 160-1;
in Portugal, 161; in Bahamas, 163-8,
*166*; President of Bahamas Red Cross
Association, *166*; returns to France
after war, 169; house in Bois de

Boulogne, 169; at Paris Horse Show
(1949), *171*; at Portofino, *174*; life at
Mill, 175-80, *176*; learns French,
180; visits to Venice, 180-1;
memoirs, 181-3; dancing at Hotel
Plaza, *185*; Horst's portraits, *189*, *190*;
entertaining, 192; at unveiling of
plaque to Queen Mary, *193*; in 1959,
*194*; visits to London, *196*; as
godmother, *200*; with Queen Mother
after Duke's funeral, *206*; at
Buckingham Palace after Duke's
death, 207; old age, 207-11; returns
to France after Duke's funeral, *208*;
dinner party (1975), *208*; letters
following television serial, 210
Windsor, Duke of (*for earlier entries see*
Edward, Prince; Edward, Prince of
Wales; Edward VIII): leaves for
France after Abdication, 122;
telephone calls to George VI, 127;
wedding, *133-4*, 136-9;
honeymoon, 140, *142*; expectation of
return to England, 140, 143; visit to
Germany (1937), 143-8, *145*, *147*;
lunch with Goering, 144; meets
Hitler, 144-8, *147*; and George VI,
149; life at La Croë, 150-3; Paris
house, 153; programme for day, 153;
at War Office, *154*; returns to England
at outbreak of war, 155; choice of
jobs, 155; assigned to British
Military Mission, Vincennes, 155-6;
on *HMS Kelly*, *156*; in France (1939),
*159*; leaves France for Spain, 160-1;
in Portugal, 161; Spanish
suggestion of return to Throne,
161-2; Governor of Bahamas, 163-8,
*164*, *166*; returns to France after war,
169; house in Bois de Boulogne, 169;
with Queen Mary (1945), *171*; with
Churchill at Antibes, *173*; at
Portofino, *174*; garden at Mill, 175;
life at Mill, 175-80, *176*; visits to
Venice, 180-1; financial investments,
181; memoirs, 181-3; golfing at
Deauville, *183*; publication of
memoirs, *184*; dancing at Hotel
Plaza, *185*; with Jimmy Donahue at
Portofino, *186*; at unveiling of
plaque to Queen Mary, *193*; visit to
London, *196*; operations for
ballooning artery and detached
retina, 198; after operation for
detached retina, *199*; death, 201-7;
funeral, *206*, 207; lying-in-state, 207

York, Duchess of, *see* Princess May
York, Duke of (Prince George), *see*
George, Prince
York, Duke of (Prince Albert), *see*
Bertie, Prince
York Cottage, 32, *33*, 34, 38
York House, 63, 86